Best-Loved Designers

WEEKEND QUILTS
& CRAFTS

A Sampler of 65 Easy Quilts and Coordinating Projects from America's Top Designers

Landauer Books

BEST-LOVED DESIGNERS COLLECTION:
WEEKEND QUILTS & CRAFTS

Copyright © 2004 by Landauer Corporation

This book was designed and produced by
Landauer Books
A division of Landauer Corporation
12251 Maffit Road, Cumming, Iowa 50061

President and Publisher: Jeramy Lanigan Landauer
Director of Operations: Kitty Jacobson
Editor in Chief: Becky Johnston
Creative Director: Laurel Albright
Art Director: Linda Bender
Technical Editors: Patty Barrett, Jill Reber
Photostylists: Margaret Sindelar, Debbie Burgraff
Photographers: Craig Anderson, Dennis Kennedy, Scott Little
Printed in the United States of America

ISBN: 1-890621-71-4

This book is printed on acid-free paper.

2 3 4 5 6 7 8 9 10

INTRODUCTION

Treat yourself to a fabulous sampler collection of 17 quilts and wallhangings using fresh new fabrics, dimensional appliqué, and many exciting embellishments. Then enjoy a bonus collection of 48 sew-simple coordinating projects you can finish in a flash!

The 12 contributing designers are some of the country's best fabric artists who combine the enduring charms of folk-art, romantic vintage, northwoods, and holiday collection with unique inspirations to create designs and projects for home dec as well as special occasions.

In this delightful collection, each chapter features a wonderful quilt sure to warm heart and home. Charming motifs from each of the featured wallhangings inspire a myriad of coordinating projects. Discover fun wearables, country critters, Christmas decorations, home decorative accents and much more.

To spark your imagination, you'll find dozens of fresh new projects from your favorite designers sprinkled throughout the following pages. We'll show you how to go beyond piecing with the newest and quickest way to quilt using fusible adhesive then top it all off with imaginative new ways to embellish with floss, paints, pens, buttons, beads, ribbons and yo-yos by the yard!

To help you experience the fun of working with new materials and techniques, we've provided several pages of General Instructions, Tips & Techniques and a Stitch Guide where needed.

As you begin your quilting and crafting weekend fun, confidently choose from dozens of quick-to-make fabric favorites from designers who have gained the well-deserved recognition as some of America's Best-Loved Designers!

Becky Johnston

Editor-in-Chief

TABLE OF CONTENTS

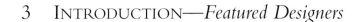

GENERAL INSTRUCTIONS

FOR EVERY PROJECT

As you gather your materials and begin each project, here are some guidelines
you may find helpful:

- The fabric called for in the materials list is 44"-wide lightweight to medium-weight cotton unless otherwise specified.
- Scraps of fabric are intended to be those you have on hand. If you don't have a particular color or pattern in your scrap basket, you'll only need to purchase ⅛ yard pieces or fat quarters.
- Since many of these projects are decorative items, it's not necessary to prewash the fabrics. Prewash fabrics for any piece that will be laundered.
- Cut strips and rectangles with a rotary cutter for speed and accuracy.
- Sew all seams with a ¼" seam allowance unless noted otherwise. After stitching, press seam allowances to one side, usually toward the darker fabric.

QUICK-SEW APPLIQUÉ
TRACE, APPLY FUSIBLE WEB, CUT, AND FUSE

- Use regular-weight fusible web unless directed otherwise in the materials list. Regular and lightweight fusibles have a lighter coating of adhesive, and the appliqué pieces should be hand- or machine-stitched after fusing. Heavyweight fusible web is for projects where the appliqué pieces are not stitched.
- Place the fusible web, paper side up, over the appliqué patterns. Trace the patterns. (The patterns are the reverse of the finished project.) Cut the fusible web about ⅛" outside the traced line (Diagram A). To save time, trace all patterns to be cut from one fabric about ¼" apart from each other on the fusible web. Cut around the outside of the grouped patterns.
- Fuse the pattern to the wrong side of the fabric. Cut out on the traced lines (Diagram B). Transfer any dashed placement lines to the fabric.
- Peel off the paper backing. Position the appliqué on the background fabric, overlapping the pieces at the dashed lines; fuse in place (Diagram C).

FINISHING THE WALLHANGING OR QUILT
LAYERING

- Cut the backing and batting several inches larger than the quilt top.
- Lay the backing wrong side up on a flat surface. Secure the edges with tape. Center the batting over the backing, smoothing it flat. Position the finished top on the batting.
- Hand-baste or safety-pin the layers together about every 4", beginning in the middle and working to the edges. Trim the batting and backing even with or ¼" beyond the edges of the quilt top.

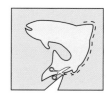

DIAGRAM A

DIAGRAM B

DIAGRAM C

QUILTING

BY MACHINE

- Sew with a fairly long straight stitch. A walking foot attachment helps keep layers even and makes quilting easier. To change direction, stop with the needle in the fabric, lift the presser foot, and pivot the fabric on the needle.
- For intricate designs, use an embroidery foot attachment and lower the feed dogs. Use an embroidery hoop to help keep the fabric stretched.

DIAGRAM D

BY HAND

- Thread the needle with an 18" length of quilting thread and tie a small knot at the end. Insert the needle through the quilt top and into the batting, about 1" from where you will begin quilting. Bring the needle up at the beginning of the quilting line, giving the thread a gentle tug to pull the knot through the top and hide it in the batting.
- Take several small, even running stitches at a time. To end a line of stitching, make a small knot close to the fabric. Insert the needle into the fabric and bring it out again about 1" from the end of the stitching. Pop the knot through the top layer into the batting, and cut the thread.

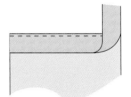

DIAGRAM E

ADDING A HANGING SLEEVE

- The sleeve is added after quilting is completed but before the binding is added. Follow these instructions to make a 2½"-wide sleeve, a good size for most wallhangings. First, cut a strip of fabric 5½" inches wide and 1" shorter than the width of the quilt.
- Press under ½", then ½" again on each short end; machine stitch the hem. Fold the strip in half lengthwise, wrong sides together, and press. Pin the strip to the top back edge of the quilt, with raw edges even (Diagram D). Stitch with a ¼" seam allowance. The raw edges will be covered by the quilt binding.
- After the binding is stitched to the quilt, smooth and pin the hanging sleeve. Whipstitch the sleeve's folded edge in place.

DIAGRAM F

BINDING

- Sew the binding strips together into one long strip. Fold the strip in half lengthwise, wrong sides together, and press.
- With raw edges even, pin the binding to the quilt top, leaving several inches loose at the beginning. Sew with a ¼" seam allowance.
- At the corner, fold the binding up at a 45° angle (Diagram E), then down at a 90° angle. Sew from the top (Diagram F), continuing along the edges to 6" from the beginning. Overlap; trim ends to ½". Open the binding, sew the ends together, refold the binding and finish sewing to the top.
- Turn the binding to the back so it just covers the stitching. Whipstitch the folded edge in place, making mitered corners on the back (Diagram G).

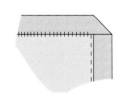

DIAGRAM G

Sally Korte & Alice Strebel

FRIENDSHIP IN BLOOM

There are probably as many different types of friendships as there are reasons for forming them. We develop relationships with neighbors, business colleagues, garden group members, etc.

Then there are friendships that are deeper, and longer-lasting. These are friends with whom you share not only an interest or an activity but a way of life and a system of values. These are kindred spirits—and who better to design a collection celebrating friendship than two women who named their business for their own relationship?

Sally Korte and Alice Strebel have been friends and business partners—Kindred Spirits—for over ten years. Their business developed, in part, because friends asked them to create patterns for their distinctive clothing. They continue to meet people who share their outlook on life. "When we teach we always find immediate friends in our classes," Sally says. "They already feel they know our hearts because of our work." This comes as no surprise to Sally and Alice, who describe kindred spirits as "those people who are friends even if they don't know each other yet, and who will remain friends even if they never see each other again."

Let your friends know how much they mean to you by creating one of these friendship gifts. Vary the embellishing, making each one a personal token of affection.

MATERIALS

- ¼ yard of burlap or light tan fabric for background
- Assorted large scraps for pocket, pieced borders, heart appliqué, and ruched flower
- ⅜ yard of fabric for backing
- Gray, green, black, gold, blue, and red embroidery floss
- 13" x 21" piece of thin cotton batting
- ⅝" button
- Fade-away fabric marker

Finished size 12" x 20"

CUTTING

1. From the burlap or tan fabric, cut the following rectangles: 4½" x 10½" (A), 2½" x 4½" (B), 3½" x 4½" (C), 4½" x 6½" (D), 5½" x 8½" (E), and 4½" x 5½" (F).

2. From the assorted scraps, cut two pockets (one will be the lining) and one heart using the patterns on page 17. Cut one 1¼" x 12" strip for the ruched flower. For the pieced border, cut 1½"-wide strips ranging from 3½" to 6½" in length. (You will need approximately 101" of pieced border.)

3. From the backing fabric, cut a 13" x 21" rectangle.

ASSEMBLY

1. Using the fade-away marker and referring to the photo as needed, write the phrases "Friends, Like Flowers, Bloom Longest in Our Memories," "Forget Me Not," and "Rosemary for Remembrance" on the appropriate rectangles. Transfer the bee, ladybug, beehive and flower designs from pages 17-18. Use three strands of floss to satin-stitch the bee and lady bug bodies and to make the flowers with a lazy

daisy stitch. Use four strands of floss to backstitch all remaining stitching.

2. Blanket-stitch the heart to the C rectangle, leaving the edges raw.

3. To make the ruched flower, press under ¼" on both long edges of the 1¼" x 12" strip. Sew loose running stitches from fold to fold at a 45-degree angle, as shown in Diagram A. Gather the thread up as tightly as possible as you go. Evenly distribute the gathers and knot the end. Form a tight circle at one end, and curl the strip into a tight spiral, overlapping the edges, and tacking it as you go along. Stitch the flower in place on the D rectangle.

DIAGRAM A

4. Place the pocket and pocket lining right sides together and stitch around the outside edges, leaving an opening for turning. Trim the seam allowances and turn right side out through the opening. Press the flap toward the front of the pocket, and stitch the button in place to hold the flap down. Position the pocket on the E rectangle so that it is centered from side to side and ¾" from the bottom edge. Blanket-stitch in place using three strands of floss.

5. Lay out the completed rectangles, referring to Diagram B for placement. Sew the 1½"-wide strips together end-to-end, and add these pieced borders between the rectangles as shown. Sew border strips to the top and bottom edges, and then to the sides.

6. Trim the backing and batting to match the completed quilt top. Place the quilt top right sides together with the

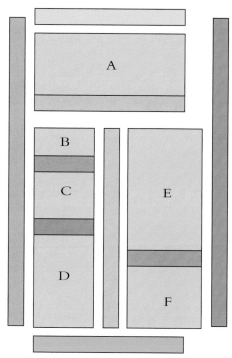

DIAGRAM B

backing, and then place the batting on top; pin. Sew the three layers together, leaving an opening for turning. Trim the seam allowances, and turn right side out through the opening. Sew the opening closed.

7. Quilt through the center of the pieced borders using three strands of floss and long running stitches.

Forget-Me-Not Pillow

10" x 16"

MATERIALS

- ½ yard of print fabric for pillow
- ¼ yard of burlap for sleeve
- Assorted scraps for ruched flower and pieced binding
- Green, gold, blue, and gray embroidery floss
- Polyester stuffing
- Fade-away fabric marker

CUTTING

1. From the print fabric, cut a 16" x 20" rectangle. From the burlap, cut a 7½" x 20" rectangle.
2. From the scraps, cut a 1¼" x 12" strip for the ruched flower. Cut fourteen 1¾" x 3½" pieces for the binding.

ASSEMBLY

1. Fold the print fabric in half cross-wise, right sides together, so that it measures 16" x 10". Sew the long seam, leaving a 3" opening near the center. Sew the two side seams. Trim the seam allowances and turn

right side out through the opening. Stuff the pillow and sew the opening closed.

2. Sew seven binding pieces together end to end to make one long strip. Fold the binding in half lengthwise, wrong sides together, and press. Repeat with the remaining seven binding pieces.

3. Pin the binding strips to the right side of the 7½" x 20" burlap rectangle, aligning the raw edges. Sew with ¼" seam allowances, and press the binding toward the edges. Handstitch along the outside edges with embroidery floss and long running stitches.

4. Fold the rectangle in half crosswise, right sides together, so that it measures 7½" x 10". Stitch the seam, and turn right side out.

5. Using a fade-away marker, transfer the embroidery design onto the pillow sleeve and write the words "Forget Me Not." Backstitch the stems, leaves, and words using six strands of floss. The forget-me-nots are lazy daisy stitches and the flower centers are French knots, both stitched with three strands of floss.

6. Make the ruched flower following the directions in Step 3 of the Quick-Sew Wallhanging Assembly instructions. Stitch the completed flower at the top of the stem. Slip the sleeve onto the pillow.

Busy Bee Doll

6" x 10" sitting

MATERIALS

- ⅜ yard of black check fabric for arms and legs
- ¼ yard of gold plaid fabric for body
- ⅛ yard or scrap of black fabric for head
- Polyester stuffing
- Black embroidery floss
- Two ½" gold buttons
- Four ½" black buttons
- Straw hat
- Black paint
- 2¼ yards of dark wire

ASSEMBLY

1. Using the patterns on pages 19-21, trace and cut out two heads from black fabric. Cut one body front and two body backs from gold plaid fabric.

2. Fold the black check fabric in half, right sides together. Trace the arm and leg patterns twice onto the doubled fabric. Sew on the traced lines, leaving the straight ends open.

3. Cut out the arms and legs and turn right side out. Stuff the hands and feet to the line indicated on the pattern. Tie black floss knots at the wrists and the ankles.

4. Place the two back pieces right sides together, and sew the center back seam from the neck edge to the dot marked on the pattern.

5. Place the back right sides together with a head piece, aligning the straight edges at the neck. Sew together across the neck edge. Repeat with the front and the second head piece.

6. Position the arms 1½" below the neck seam on the body front, gather the fabric slightly and baste. Position the legs approximately ¼" on either side of the center front; gather slightly and baste.

7. Pin the back and front right sides together, matching the neck seams. Place the arms inside, out of the seam area, but leave the legs dangling out the bottom. Sew around the body from one leg, up around the head and down to the other leg. Leave open at the bottom where the legs protrude.

8. Turn right side out and stuff firmly. Sew the opening closed. Sew on the gold button eyes, and sew a black button at each wrist and ankle.

9. Cut a 9" length of wire and set aside.

To make the wings, bend the remaining length of wire back and forth into three loops on each side of the bee, making each loop about 6" long. Pinch the loops together in the center and stitch to the back of the bee about 1¼" below the neck seam.

10. Paint the hat black and "scrunch" it to make it look old. Poke the 9" piece of wire through the top of the hat and curl the ends to make antennae.

Gardener's Tote Bag

Approximately 10" x 14" x 5"

MATERIALS

- ⅞ yard of burlap for bag and lining
- ⅜ yard of print fabric for large pockets
- ⅛ yard each or large scraps of two black plaid fabrics for straps
- Assorted scraps for pocket trim, small pocket, and ruched flowers
- Green, black, and light gold embroidery floss
- Seven assorted buttons
- Fade-away fabric marker

CUTTING

1. From the burlap, cut two 20" x 26" rectangles.
2. From the print fabric, cut two 5½" x 10½" rectangles for the pocket fronts and two 7" x 12" rectangles for the linings.

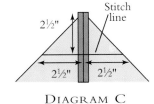

2½" ← → 2½" | 2½" →
Stitch line

DIAGRAM C

3. From each plaid fabric, cut two 1¾" x 44" strips.
4. From the scraps, cut two 1¼" x 12" strips for ruched flowers, and one pocket and pocket lining from the pattern on page 17. Cut four 1" x 10½" and four 1" x 7" strips for the trim on the large pockets.

ASSEMBLING THE BAG

1. Fold a 20" x 26" burlap rectangle in half crosswise, right sides together, so that it measures 20" x 13". Stitch the two sides using a ½" seam allowance.
2. At one lower corner, fold the bag as shown in Diagram C, centering the seam on the folded corner. Measure 2½" in from the corner and mark a stitching line. Pin, then stitch along the marked line. Repeat on the opposite corner. Turn the bag right side out.
3. In the same manner, fold and stitch the second rectangle, but leave an opening in one side seam for turning. Stitch the corners as described in Step 2. This will be the bag's lining.
4. With right sides facing, tuck the bag inside the lining, aligning the top edges. Stitch around the top of the bag. Turn the bag and the lining right side out through the opening in the lining. Tuck the lining inside the bag and stitch the opening closed. To keep the lining from shifting, tack the bag and lining together at the bottom corners.
5. To make the straps, sew each pair of 1¾"-wide strips end-to-end to make two 84"-long strips. Place the strips right sides together, and sew both long sides with a ¼" seam allowance. Turn the tube right side out and press.
6. The straps begin and end at the bottom of the bag. Pin one end of the strip to the flat bottom of the bag,

with the outside edge of the strip approximately 3" in from the edge of the bag. Pinning as you go, bring the strip up the side of the bag, leave a 17" loop for the handle, and come back down the same side, making sure the strap is again 3" from the outside edge. Take the strip across the bottom of the bag and up the other side, allow a 17" loop, and bring it down the same side, back to the starting point at the bottom. Fold in the raw edges on both ends, and stitch in place. Make any necessary adjustments and make sure the handles are exactly the same length. When you are satisfied, blanket-stitch both edges of the straps using three strands of floss.

FINISHING

1. Make the small pocket as described in Step 4 of the Quick-Sew Wallhanging instructions. Position the completed pocket between the straps on one side of the bag, and blanket-stitch in place.

2. Accent the bag with embroidery as desired, referring to Step 1 of the Quick-Sew Wallhanging Assembly instructions. On the bag shown, the words "Rosemary for Remembrance" along with two ruched flowers and a bee were added between the straps on one side. "Friends, Like Flowers, Bloom Longest in Our Memories" was stitched around the top edge.

3. To make the large pockets, begin by sewing the 1" x 10½" strips to the top and bottom edges of the pocket fronts, using a ¼" seam allowance. Sew the 1" x 7" strips to the sides. Place the pocket fronts right sides together with the linings, and stitch with a ¼" seam allowance, leaving an opening for turning. Turn right side out and stitch

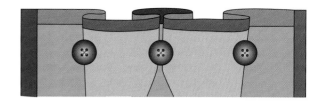

the opening closed. Position a pocket on each end of the bag, and blanket-stitch in place using three strands of embroidery floss.

4. Pleat the fabric at the top of each pocket as shown in Diagram D, gathering the fabric as much or as little as desired, and sew a button at each pleat. The pleats will have the effect of gathering the sides of the bag.

Friendship Card & Envelope

4½" x 7"

MATERIALS

- ¼ yard each of two print fabrics for envelope
- Large scraps of light and print fabrics for card and tag
- Scraps of red, blue, and gold fabric for flowers
- Green and brown embroidery floss
- Fabric stiffener
- 6" piece of wire
- One ⅝" and two ½" buttons
- Fade-away fabric marker

CUTTING

1. From the print fabrics, cut two 5¾" x 17" rectangles.

2. From the scraps, cut one 4" x 6" piece and one 1¾" x 3" piece of light fabric, and two 5" x 7" pieces of print fabric.

ASSEMBLY

1. Place the two 5" x 7" rectangles right sides together. Sew all around the outside edges. Trim the seam allowances. Carefully cut a small slit through the front layer of fabric. Turn right side out and press. Set aside.

2. Using the fade-away marker, transfer the design from page 18 onto the 4" x 6" rectangle. Backstitch the words and stems using two or three strands of floss. Cut the flower circles and attach them with green floss French knots.

3. Using two strands of floss and long running stitches, sew the stitched piece to the print background. Poke two small holes at the top and insert the wire; twist the ends to hold it in place. Stiffen the greeting card following

the manufacturer's directions.

4. To make the envelope, place the two 5¾" x 17" rectangles right sides together. Place the pattern for the envelope point at one end of the fabric and cut around it. Sew around the edges, leaving an opening for turning. Trim the seam allowances. Turn right side out through the opening. Press.

5. Cut a 1" x 7" strip of any fabric. Turn in ¼" at each end, and pin to the lining side of the point, right sides together and raw edges even. Stitch with a ¼" seam allowance. Fold the binding to the outside, turn in the raw edge, and blindstitch in place.

6. Fold the envelope right sides together, bringing the bottom end up just to where the point begins. Pin the sides together, and machine-stitch very close to the edge. Turn the envelope right side out. Make a buttonhole in the pointed end and sew the ⅝" closure button in place.

7. Transfer the design for the words and flower onto the 1¾" x 3" rectangle. Backstitch the words and flower stem using two strands of floss. Cut a tiny circle of fabric for the flower, and attach in place with a French knot. Sew the buttons near the bottom of the envelope. Cut a buttonhole slit on each side of the patch, and button it onto the envelope.

2" x 3"

MATERIALS

- Two 4" x 5" pieces of burlap
- Scrap of fusible web
- Polyester stuffing
- Black and gold embroidery floss
- Pinback
- Fade-away fabric marker

ASSEMBLY

1. Trace the heart pattern, below, onto the center of both burlap pieces. Transfer the bee design onto the center of one of the traced hearts.

2. Using three strands of floss, satin-stitch the black and gold stripes of the bee's body. Backstitch the wings in black.

3. Cut out the two hearts. Place the front and back right sides together and sew all around the outside edge. Carefully cut a slit through just the back layer of fabric, and turn right side out. Stuff.

4. Iron a small piece of fusible web onto a scrap of fabric. Cut a small heart from the fabric and fuse it onto the back of the stitched heart to cover the slit. Sew on the pinback.

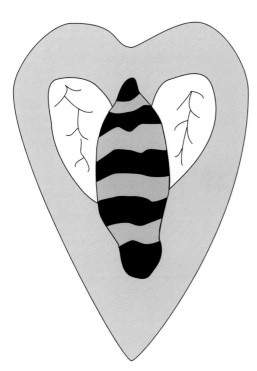

BEE PIN PATTERN

RUCHED FLOWER

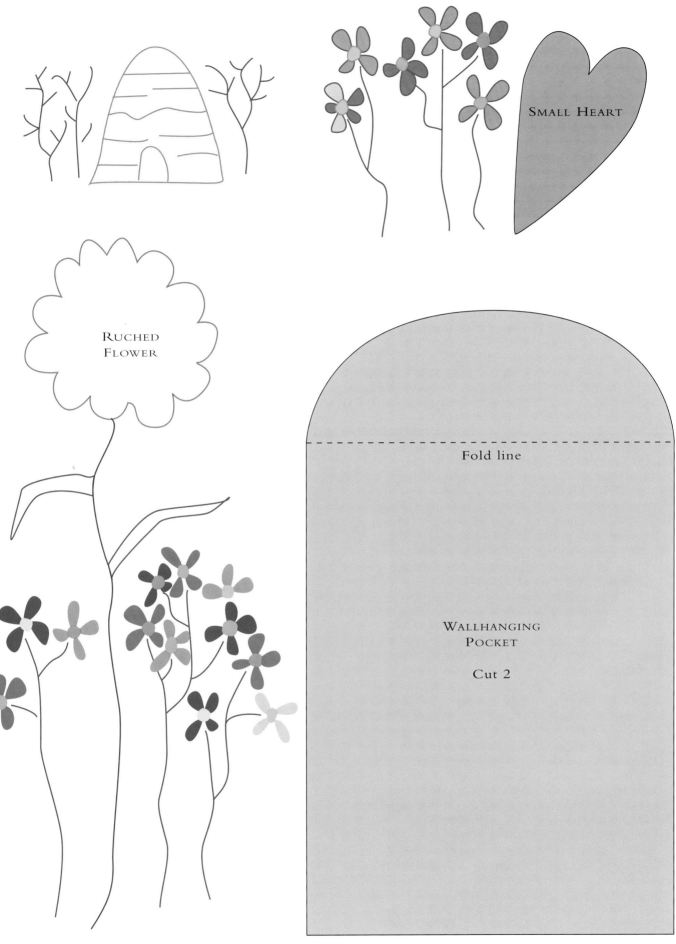

SMALL HEART

RUCHED
FLOWER

Fold line

WALLHANGING
POCKET

Cut 2

you're so thoughtful you're so kind A truer friend I'll never find

To you from Me

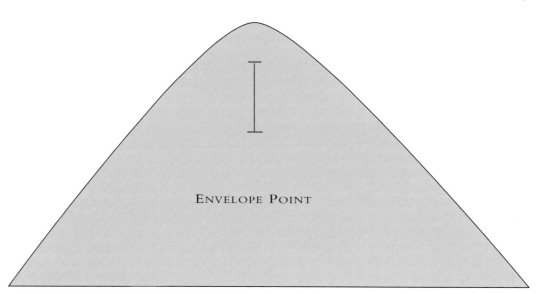

ENVELOPE POINT

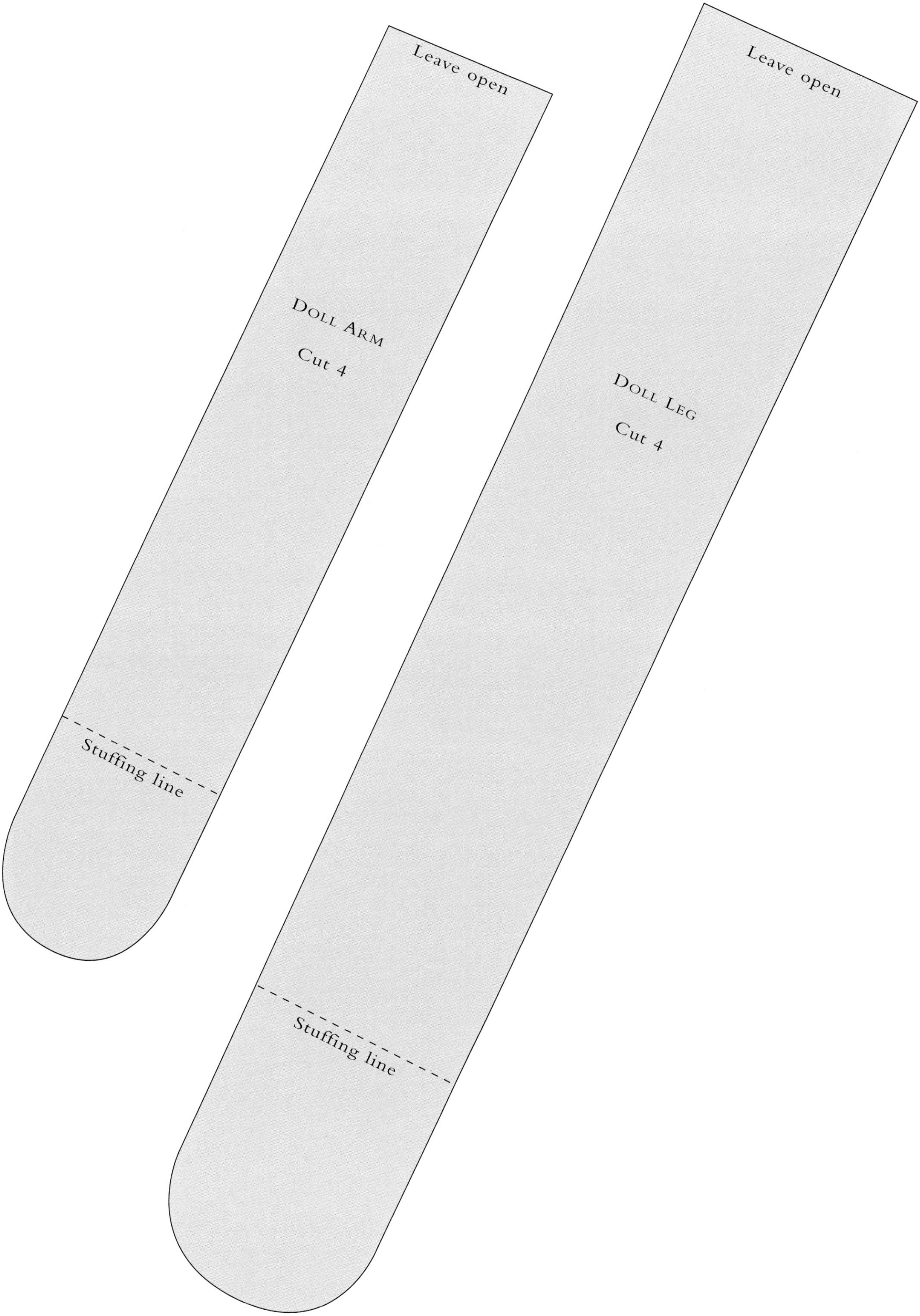

Leave open

Leave open

DOLL ARM

Cut 4

DOLL LEG

Cut 4

Stuffing line

Stuffing line

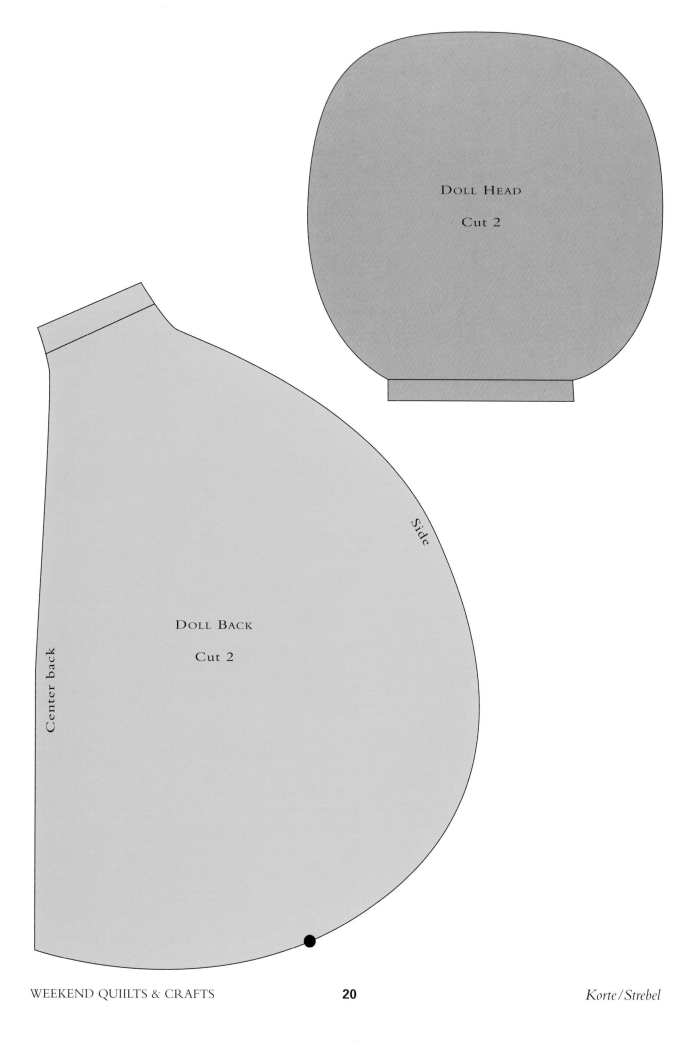

DOLL HEAD

Cut 2

Side

DOLL BACK

Cut 2

Center back

DOLL FRONT

Kris Kerrigan

A BUSY HEN'S KITCHEN

Easter at the Kerrigan's begins at dawn when their roosters crow, announcing the start of the traditional egg hunt! When the children were young, Kris explains, a note to the Easter Bunny asked that the egg hunt take place in two rooms, with the boys in one and the girls in another. Even now that they're older, this competition is still keen.

Dinner is the major event of the day, and preparations begin after church services. Everyone helps dye the eggs—boiling and shelling and dipping them in mugs of dye. Kris devils yolks and arranges the colorful halves on a platter, making a beautiful presentation. Her grandfather was a chef and her mother enjoyed creating unique dishes, so preparing a special holiday meal is a family tradition.

That tradition, and Kris' own hens, inspired her to create the Busy Hen's Kitchen collection. Kris and her daughter, Rachel, raise chickens on their Iowa farm. One breed, the Araucanas, lay eggs in shades from turquoise to deep olive. Collecting their eggs, Kris says, "is like celebrating Easter every day!" She hopes the Busy Hen's quilt, with its personalized eggs, will become a keepsake in your family.

MATERIALS

- 1½ yards of green solid fabric for backing, large background, and appliqués
- ½ yard of yellow plaid or print fabric for borders, wings, and appliqués
- ⅓ yard of striped fabric for borders, aprons, and appliqués
- ½ yard of blue print fabric for binding, background, and appliqués
- ¼ yard each of one blue and three green print fabrics for backgrounds
- ⅛ yard of blue check fabric for background, binding, and appliqués
- ⅛ yard each or scraps of cream, blue, pink, and yellow solid fabrics for pieced eggs and appliqués
- ⅛ yard or scraps of pink print fabric for nests
- 36" square of batting
- Fusible web
- White, pink, yellow, blue, and green embroidery floss
- ⅝ yard of ¼" green ribbon
- Six ¼" buttons
- Fade-away fabric marker
- Black fine-point permanent marker

Quick-Sew Wallhanging

Finished size 32" square

CUTTING

1. From the green solid fabric, cut one 36" square for the back, one 14" square (A), and three 2½" x 3½" rectangles (F).
2. From the yellow plaid fabric, cut two 1½" x 29¼" strips (O), three 1½" x 27¼" strips (N), one 1½" x 19" strip (K), one 1½" x 15" strip (C), one 1½" x 14" strip (B), and three 1½" x 8¾" strips (M).
3. From the striped fabric, cut two 2" x 32¼" strips (Q), two 2" x 29¼" strips (P), and three 3¼" x 5" rectangles (aprons).
4. From the blue check fabric, cut one 1" x 18" strip (J), one 1" x 17½" strip (I), one 1" x 15½" strip (E), one 1" x 15" strip (D), one 2½" square (H), and forty 1" squares (G).
5. From the blue print fabric, cut four 2" x 44" strips for binding and one 8¾" square (L).
6. From the blue and green print fabrics, cut one blue and three green 8¾" squares (L).

23

Kris Kerrigan

7. From the cream solid fabric, cut one 1¾" x 9" rectangle ripped into eighteen ½"-wide pieces for straw. From the pink solid fabric, cut three 2½" x 3½" rectangles (F), and from the yellow and blue solid fabrics cut two 2½" x 3½" rectangles each (F).

8. Refer to the General Instructions on page 6 to trace, apply fusible web to, and cut the following appliqué pieces: From the cream solid fabric, cut nine small eggs from the pattern on page 31; one 4¼" square, cut diagonally for two hen bodies; one 2¼" square, cut diagonally for two wings; and one 1¾" x 2½" rectangle for Rapid Rabbit's note.

9. From the yellow solid fabric, cut two 4¼" squares, cut diagonally for four hen bodies; one 2¼" x 3¼" rectangle; one mug handle and one spoon handle from the patterns on page 31.

10. From the yellow plaid fabric, cut two 2¼" squares, cut diagonally for four wings.

11. From the pink solid fabric, cut one 2¼" x 3¼" rectangle; three 1½" squares, cut diagonally for six hen combs/wattles; and one mug handle and one spoon handle from the patterns on page 31.

12. From the pink print, cut three 2¼" x 5" rectangles for nests.

13. From assorted fabrics, cut 26 small eggs from the pattern on page 31.

APPLIQUÉ AND ASSEMBLY

1. Refer to the photograph and follow the instructions at right for placement of the appliqués. After fusing the appliqués in position, use embroidery floss to blanket-stitch by hand or machine around them.

2. Center and fuse the nests at the bottom

of the green L squares; blanket-stitch. Center and fuse a yellow print hen wing on three of the yellow bodies. Fuse a comb/wattle and a body by each nest. Place six pieces of straw on each nest and fuse three eggs on top to hold them in place. Stitch around the appliqué pieces, leaving the ends of the straw free. Sew on button eyes.

3. Position a mug handle ⅜" from the side of each blue L square, and place the mug so that it slightly overlaps the handle; fuse. Center and fuse the two white hen wings on the two white bodies. Fuse a comb/wattle and a body to each blue L square, placing the tail 3¾" and the beak 5¾" from the bottom of the square; stitch. Fuse and stitch the pink spoon handle at the top edge of the yellow mug, with the handle overlapping the hen's body and touching the wing. Repeat for the

yellow spoon handle above the pink mug. Fuse a print egg (matching the color of the mug) to the top of each mug, overlapping the spoon handle slightly; stitch.

4. Cut two 6½" lengths of ribbon and tie each into a bow. Tack the bows below the chicken wings. To make the aprons, press under ¼", then ¼" again along one long edge of the two 3¼" x 5" striped rectangles. Gather this edge with running stitches of embroidery floss. Tack one end to the hen's breast just below the spoon handle and the other end beside the bow. Embroider tail feathers, legs, and toes in long stitch or back stitch. Add button eyes.

5. Repeat instructions above for the yellow hen on the large background with one change: this hen holds an egg slightly tucked under her wing. Fuse this egg to the body before fusing the wing. With the black permanent marker, write "Call Rapid Rabbit's Delivery Service 555-1234" on the 1¾" x 2½" rectangle of cream fabric. Fuse to the right side of the background above the hen; stitch. Long-stitch a pin shank and add a French knot for a pin head. Fuse and stitch the pile of eggs to the left side of the background, placing colors randomly.

6. To make the name eggs, place four squares (G) on the corners of each rectangle (F) as shown in Diagram A; stitch as indicated by the dotted lines. Fold each G toward the corner and press; trim the excess seam allowance. Sew the eggs into two rows of five eggs each. Sew the H square to the end of one row.

7. Assemble the quilt top following Diagrams B (below), and C (next page), and these instructions: Sew B to

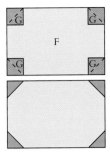

DIAGRAM A

the right side of A, then sew C to the bottom of the A unit, D to the right side, then E to the bottom. Sew the row of eggs without the H square to the bottom of the A unit, then sew the other row of eggs to the right side. Sew I to the right side of the A unit, J to the bottom, then K to the left side.

8. Stitch a horizontal M sashing between two L blocks; add to the left side of the A unit. Sew vertical M sashings between the remaining L blocks, and sew N sashings to the top and bottom of this row. Sew this section to the top of the L/A unit, and add another N sashing to the bottom of the L/A unit. Sew the O sashings to the sides. Add the P borders to the top and bottom, and the Q borders to the sides.

FINISHING

1. With the fade-away marker, write your family members' names centered on the name eggs. Embroider the

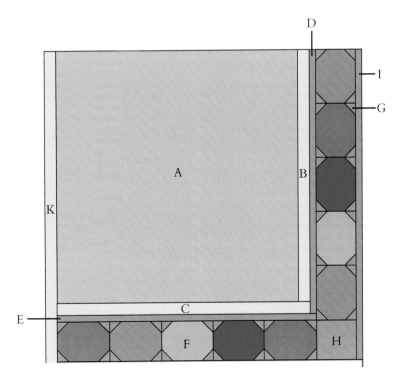

DIAGRAM B

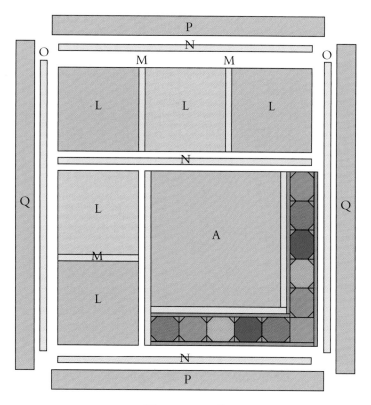

DIAGRAM C

names in backstitch or chain-stitch. In the same manner, add the color names on the mugs.

2. Refer to the General Instructions on page 7 to layer the wallhanging, then quilt as desired. Trim the edges of the layers even.

3. Prepare the binding strips and a hanging sleeve as directed on page 7. Referring to the General Instructions for mitered corners, sew the binding in place using a ¼" seam allowance. Turn the binding to the back and whipstitch in place.

Finished size 12½" x 40"

MATERIALS

- ¾ yard of yellow plaid fabric for backing, hens, and inner border
- ⅜ yard of blue print fabric for outer border
- ¼ yard of green solid fabric for background
- ¼ yard of yellow print fabric for hen wings
- Assorted scraps or ⅛ yard each of pink, yellow, and blue fabrics for eggs, combs, wattles, and beaks
- 14" x 43" piece of batting
- Fusible web
- Pink, white, blue, green, and yellow embroidery floss
- Fade-away fabric marker
- Two ½" buttons

CUTTING

1. From the yellow plaid fabric, cut one 13" x 29½" rectangle for runner back, two 9⅜" squares for hen bodies (front and back), two 1" x 24½" strips and two 1" x 9½" strips for inner border.

2. From the blue print fabric, cut two 2¼" x 25¾" strips and two 2¼" x 13" strips for outer border.

3. From the green fabric, cut one 8½" x 24¾" rectangle for the background.

4. From the yellow print fabric, cut two 6" squares for wings and two 2½" squares for beaks.

5. From the pink fabric scraps, cut two 2½" squares for combs, and two

2" squares cut diagonally for four wattle triangles.

6. Refer to the General Instructions on page 6 to trace, apply fusible web to, and cut the following appliqué pieces: From pink, yellow, and blue prints, cut 11 medium eggs from the pattern on page 31.

ASSEMBLY

1. Position and fuse the eggs randomly in the green background. Stitch around the eggs with embroidery floss and blanket stitches.

2. Sew the long 1" inner border strips to the sides of the background, and sew the shorter 1" strips to the ends. Sew the long 2¼" border strips to the sides, and sew the shorter strips to the ends.

3. With a fade-away marker, mark the two 2½" beak squares with a diagonal line. Place each square right sides together with a body square, as shown in Diagram D(1). Sew on marked line. Trim seam allowance to ¼" (2). Press beak toward corner (3). Cut each square diagonally, forming four body triangles (4).

4. Sew two wattle triangles right sides together on the short sides as shown in Diagram E. Turn right side out and press. Sew the wattle triangles near the

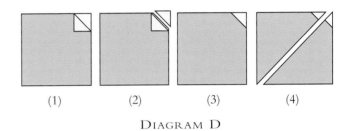

(1)   (2)   (3)   (4)

DIAGRAM D

DIAGRAM E

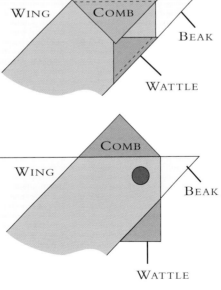

WING   COMB

BEAK

WATTLE

COMB

WING

BEAK

WATTLE

DIAGRAM F

beaks as shown in Diagram F.

5. Fold each of the 6" wing squares in half diagonally, then in half again to form prairie points; press. Repeat for each 2½" comb square. Center each wing on a body triangle and stitch across the top. Sew a comb to the top of the body between the beak and the wing as shown in Diagram F.

6. Sew a completed hen front to each short end of the runner top. Sew a hen back to each short end of the backing.

7. Place the runner top wrong side down on the batting. Lay the runner backing, right sides together, on runner top. Pin all layers together. Trim the batting to the shape of the runner. Sew around the outside

edges, leaving a 5" opening on one long side for turning. Turn right side out and press; hand-stitch the opening closed.

8. Quilt around the eggs, in the borders, and on the hens' bodies, below the wing and midway between the wing and the body's bottom edges. Sew on buttons for eyes.

Chicken Place Mat

Finished size 10" x 20"

MATERIALS

- ½ yard of yellow plaid fabric for hen body
- ¼ yard of yellow print fabric for hen wings
- Scraps of pink fabric for comb and wattle and yellow striped fabric for beak
- 15" square of batting
- One ⅝" button
- Fade-away fabric marker

CUTTING

1. From the yellow plaid fabric, cut one 15" square for hen body.
2. From the yellow print fabric, cut one 8¾" square, cut diagonally for two wing triangles.
3. From the pink fabric, cut one 3½" square for comb, and one 2½" square, cut diagonally for two wattle triangles.
4. From the yellow striped fabric, cut one 2½" square for beak.
5. Cut the batting square diagonally in half for two triangles, though only one will be used.

ASSEMBLY

1. Referring to Step 3 of the Table Runner instructions and Diagram D, sew the beak to the body square. Refer to Step 4 of the Table Runner instructions and Diagram E for the wattle and comb construction. Sew the wing in the same fashion as the wattle, centering and stitching it to the top of the body front.

2. Place the body front wrong side down on a batting triangle. Place the body back right sides together on the body front. Stitch around the edges, leaving a 4" opening for turning. Turn right side out and press. Sew opening closed.

3. Quilt the hen body below the wing, and midway between the wing and the body's bottom edges. Sew on a button eye.

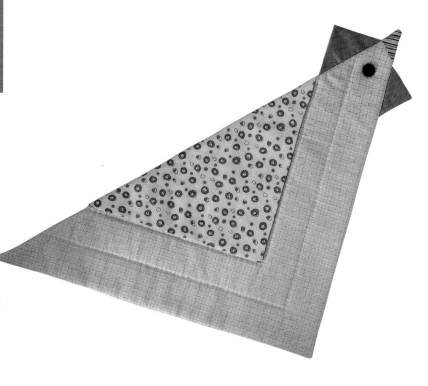

MATERIALS

For one napkin and ring

- ½ yard of yellow plaid fabric for napkin
- Scraps of blue, green, and solid cream fabrics for napkin ring
- Fusible web
- Pink and yellow embroidery floss
- ½" hook-and-loop tape
- Black fine-point permanent marker

CUTTING

1. From the yellow plaid fabric, cut one 15" square for the napkin.
2. From the green fabric, cut one 3½" x 7" strip, one 1¾" x 4" strip, and one 4" square for the napkin ring.
3. From the blue fabric, cut one 1¾" x 4" strip for the napkin ring.
4. From the solid cream fabric, cut one 1½" x 4" strip for the napkin ring.

ASSEMBLY

1. Press under ¼", then ¼" again, on each napkin edge; hem. If you prefer, serge the napkin edges.
2. Fold the 3½" x 7" strip right sides together lengthwise and sew, making a long tube. Turn right side out, center the seam on one side, and press. Turn the ends under ¼" and hem.
3. Using the black marker, print the name centered on the cream strip. Sew the strip between the two 1¾" x 4" strips. Fuse webbing between this pieced

front and the 4" square back piece.

4. Trace the large egg pattern onto the front and cut out the egg shape. Blanket-stitch around the outside edges of the egg.
5. Center the egg on the napkin ring. Using floss, sew the egg to the ring with running stitches close to the seam lines, as shown on the pattern. Cut a ½" square piece of hook-and-loop tape, and sew one side to each end of the napkin ring.

Towel

Finished size 17" x 29"

MATERIALS

- ½ yard of yellow plaid fabric for towel
- ⅛ yard each of pink and green fabrics for towel bands and appliqués
- Scraps of pink, blue, cream, and striped fabrics for appliqués
- Fusible web
- Green, cream, blue, yellow, and pink embroidery floss
- 6½" length of ¼"-wide green grosgrain ribbon
- One ¼" button
- Fade-away fabric marker

CUTTING

1. From the yellow plaid fabric, cut one 18" x 32" piece for the towel.
2. From the pink fabric, cut one 2½" x 18" strip for the towel band. From the green fabric, cut one 2" x 18" strip for towel band.

3. From the striped fabric, cut one 3¼" x 5" rectangle for the apron.

4. Refer to the General Instructions on page 6 to trace, apply fusible web to, and cut the following appliqué pieces: From the pink fabric, cut one 1½" square, cut diagonally for one comb/wattle, and one spoon handle from the pattern on page 31; from the blue fabric, cut one 2¼" x 3" rectangle, one mug handle, and one small egg; and from the cream fabric, cut one 4¼" square, cut diagonally for one hen body, and one 2¼" square, cut diagonally for one hen wing.

1. Place the pink and green strips right sides together and sew along one long side. With fade-away marker, mark a line on the yellow plaid fabric 3½" from the bottom of the towel. See Diagram G. Pin the towel band right sides together to the towel, aligning the pink strip with the marked line. Stitch with a ¼" seam allowance. Press the band down toward the bottom.

2. Press under ¼" on all edges (fold the band with the towel). Press under ¼" again and hem. Sew running stitches across the bottom of the pink band with green embroidery floss.

3. Refer to the Quick-Sew Wallhanging instructions as needed for help with positioning the appliqués and adding the apron, bow, and embroidery stitches. Center the appliqué pieces on the towel, fuse, and stitch. Construct the apron and tack on the bow. Embroider the color name on the mug, and add the hen's tail feathers and legs. Sew on a button eye.

3½"

DIAGRAM G

POT HOLDER

Fuse the hen design from the wallhanging to an 8¾" square of fabric. Blanket-stitch around the appliqués and add a button eye. Layer the stitched square with two squares of cotton batting and a backing square. (Do not use polyester batting; it will not protect your hand from heat.) Quilt the layers together and bind the edges. Sew a plastic cabone ring to the back of the pot holder at the center top.

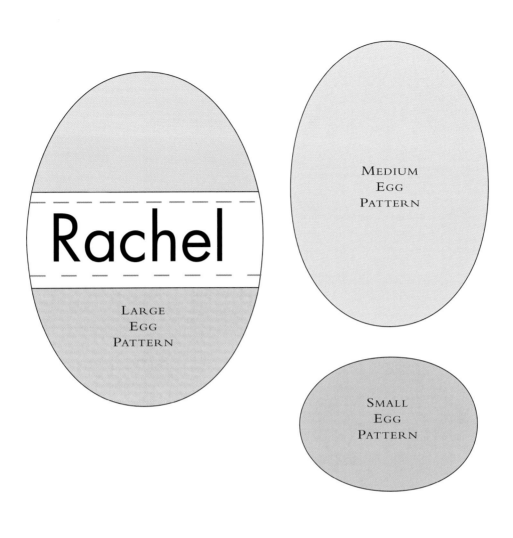

Rachel

LARGE
EGG
PATTERN

MEDIUM
EGG
PATTERN

SMALL
EGG
PATTERN

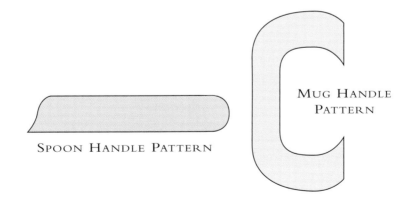

SPOON HANDLE PATTERN

MUG HANDLE
PATTERN

Janet Carija Brandt

FROM HEART TO HOME

There's something very special about coming home. Whether it's revisiting a childhood home or settling into a new one, there's a feeling of comfort, security, and belonging. Janet Brandt remembers a particular homecoming during her college years, and it was that memory that inspired her collection. "We were heading home for the holidays," Janet recalls. "It was late at night and snowing like crazy. There were several of us packed into the car, sharing the ride home, having a great time. It was hot and noisy, with the radio blaring and everyone talking at once. When I was dropped off at the foot of our long driveway, I was suddenly struck by how cold and quiet it was. As I walked up the driveway in the falling snow, I could see Christmas lights twinkling through the window. There were lights on throughout the house, and I knew everyone was home, waiting for me to arrive. It made me feel so warm and welcome, and I never forgot that special feeling. That's what coming home means to me."

Make someone you know feel special with a heartfelt gift from Janet's charming collection. Her quick wallhanging and pillow set make an ideal housewarming gift or a reminder of home for a college-bound student. Add the clever footstool for an easy, whimsical accent.

MATERIALS

- ⅝ yard of hand-dyed purple fabric for background and backing
- ¼ yard each of hand-dyed blue, green, pink, and yellow fabrics for appliqués
- ⅛ yard of pink print fabric for binding
- 20" x 21" piece of thin batting
- Lightweight fusible web
- Blue, green, pink, and yellow embroidery floss

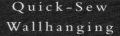

Finished size 18" x 19"

CUTTING

1. From the purple fabric, cut one 18" x 19" rectangle and one 20" x 21" rectangle.

2. From the pink print fabric, cut two 1½" x 44" strips for the binding.

3. Refer to the General Instructions on page 6 to trace, apply fusible web to, and cut out the following appliqué pieces from the patterns on pages 38-41: Three large hearts, one bird and one bird reversed, one banner 1 and one banner 1 reversed, three fleur-de-lis, two large flowers, one adult bear and one adult bear reversed, one baby bear, one table, two adult chairs, one baby chair, two adult bowls, one baby bowl, one banner 2 and one banner 2 reversed, one medium heart, letters to spell "Home Sweet Home," five small leaves, and assorted flowers and flower centers as desired. Note: For this project, the baby bear's body and head are cut and fused separately.

ASSEMBLY

1. Arrange the appliqué pieces on the 18" x 19" background rectangle. For best results, remove the backing and position all the pieces, checking their placement, before fusing any of them. Make any needed adjustments, then fuse in place.

2. Using two strands of floss, blanket-stitch around the edges of all the appliqué pieces. Blanket-stitch the arms of the adult bears as indicated by the

dashed lines on the pattern—this gives the arms the appearance of being separate pieces.

3. Layer the backing, batting, and quilt top, and baste. Using two strands of floss, echo-quilt around the shapes with rows of stitching $1/4$" apart.

4. Trim the backing and batting even with the edges of the quilt top. Prepare the binding strips and a hanging sleeve as directed in the General Instructions on page 7. Sew the binding to the quilt with a $1/4$" seam allowance. Bring the folded edge to the back and whipstitch in place.

14½" x 17", 11½" x 14", 8½" x 11"

MATERIALS

- ½ yard each of hand-dyed pink and green fabrics for background, backing, and appliqués
- ¼ yard of hand-dyed purple fabric for background, backing, and appliqués
- Large scraps of hand-dyed blue and yellow fabrics for appliqués
- Heavyweight fusible web
- Polyester stuffing
- Variegated acrylic yarn for twisted cord
- Blue, green, orange, and purple fabric markers

HOME IS WHERE THE HEART IS PILLOW

1. Cut two 15" x 17½" rectangles from the pink fabric.
2. Refer to the General Instructions on page 6 to trace, apply fusible web to, and cut out the following appliqué pieces from the patterns on pages 38-41: Two banner 1 and two banner 1 reversed, two large flowers, two large hearts, two small hearts, and letters to spell "Home Is Where The Heart Is."
3. Arrange the appliqué pieces on one of the pink fabric rectangles. For best results, remove the backing and position all the pieces, checking their placement, before fusing any of them. Make adjustments, then fuse in place.
4. Using the fabric markers, carefully outline the appliqué pieces just inside the edge of the fabric. Add "stitches" just outside the pieces.
5. Place the pillow front and back right sides together and stitch with a ¼" seam allowance, leaving an opening for turning. Turn right side out through the opening and stuff. Stitch the opening closed.
6. Measure around the outside of the pillow. Referring to the instructions on page 36, make a twisted cord to this length. Slip stitch the cording in place over the seam.

Home Sweet Home Pillow

1. Cut two 12" x 14½" rectangles from the green fabric.
2. Refer to the General Instructions on page 6 to trace, apply fusible web to, and cut out the following appliqué pieces: One bird and one bird reversed, one large heart, one small heart, two leaves, one banner 1 and one banner 1 reversed, and letters to spell "Home Sweet Home."
3. Appliqué, assemble, and finish the pillow according to the instructions in Steps 3 through 6 for the "Home Is Where The Heart Is" pillow.

I Love You Pillow

1. Cut two 9" x 11½" rectangles from purple fabric.
2. Refer to the General Instructions on page 6 to trace, apply fusible web to, and cut out the following appliqué pieces: One baby bear reversed, one small heart, one baby bench, two fleur-de-lis, letters to spell "I Love You," and assorted flowers and flower centers as desired.
3. Carefully cut just the baby bear's arms

along the dashed lines on the pattern, and slip the small heart under his paws. Fuse these pieces to the background as a unit.

4. Appliqué, assemble, and finish the pillow according to the instructions in Steps 3 through 6 for the "Home Is Where The Heart Is" pillow.

Twisted Cord

The handmade twisted cord adds a great finishing touch to the pillows and footstool. To make the cord, measure the length you'll need (around the outside of a pillow, for example) and multiply this measurement by four. Cut three pieces of yarn to that length. Hold the three lengths together and knot one end. Secure to a sturdy object. Insert the other end into the head of a Fiskars hand drill. Stand back and start to turn the crank. The yarn should be gently stretched, but not taut. Continue to crank until the yarn starts to turn back on itself. Keeping the yarn gently stretched, fold it in half, then let go. The yarn will twist back on itself, making the cord. Knot each end to hold the twist.

Approximately 11" x13" x 9"

M A T E R I A L S

- 1 yard of gold wool flannel
- ¼ yard of purple wool flannel
- ⅛ yard each or large scraps of blue, green, and pink wool flannel
- 40" square of batting
- Blue, pink, purple, and yellow embroidery floss
- 60" of twisted cord
- 10" x 12" x 7" plastic step stool
- Hot-glue gun and glue sticks

A S S E M B L Y

1. Machine-wash and -dry the wool flannel.

2. From the gold wool flannel, cut a 28" x 32" rectangle. From the purple wool flannel, cut a 9" x 12" rectangle.

3. Trim each corner of the gold rectangle as shown in Diagram A. Measure in 5½" from the corner and mark the fabric. Measure 11" along the two sides and mark. Lightly draw a line joining the three points; cut the fabric along the line. The corners will be gently curved, resulting in an oval shape.

4. Center a 9" x 12" rectangle of purple wool on the oval; pin in position. Cut assorted flowers, flower centers, and large leaves from the patterns on pages 38-41. Arrange the appliqués around the purple rectangle as desired, overlapping the edges of the rectangle all

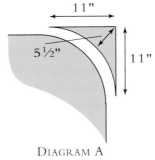

DIAGRAM A

around. Pin the appliqués in position.

5. Using two strands of floss, blanket-stitch the appliqués, then chain-stitch around the inside of the appliqués (on the purple wool) and around the outside of the design. Stitch around the outside edge of the gold wool oval using two strands of floss and a long blanket stitch.

6. Cut a strip of batting 12" x 40". Fold crosswise in half, then in half again so that it measures 12" x 10". Hot-glue the batting to the top of the step stool. Cut a 22" x 25" piece of batting. Center this piece on top of the folded batting. Gently pull the edges of the batting down, between the legs, to the underside of the step stool; hot-glue to secure. Hot-glue the batting to the outside of the legs to secure the corners.

7. Center the appliquéd oval on the step stool. Wrap the twisted cord around the stool, adjust the folds of the skirt, and pull the cord snug to hold the folds in place. Tie the cord in a bow.

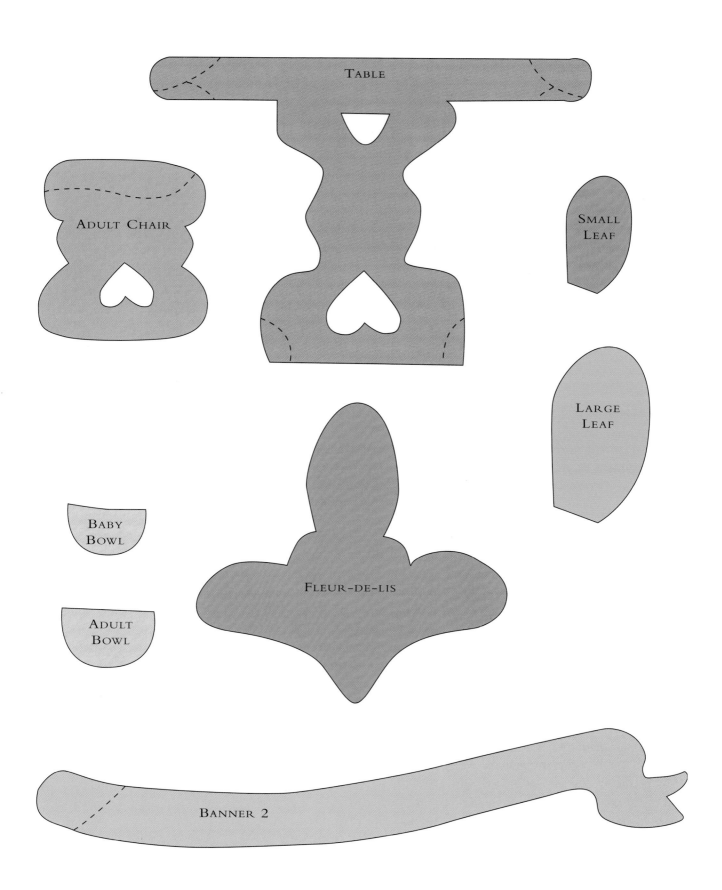

TABLE

ADULT CHAIR

SMALL
LEAF

LARGE
LEAF

BABY
BOWL

FLEUR-DE-LIS

ADULT
BOWL

BANNER 2

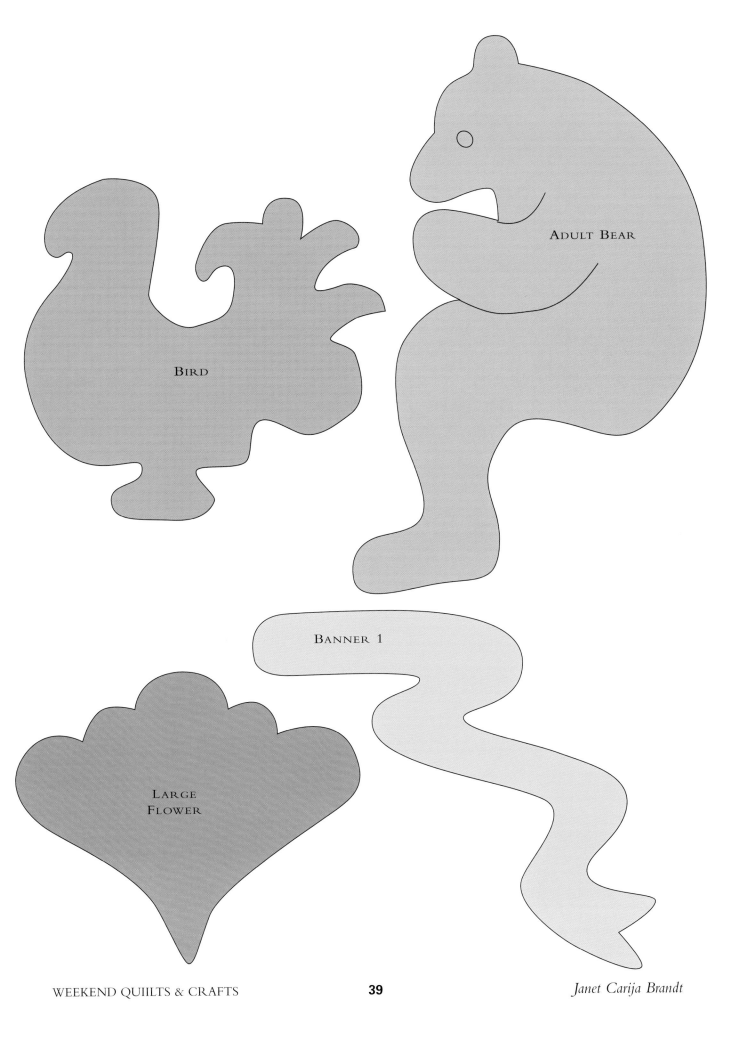

BIRD

ADULT BEAR

BANNER 1

LARGE
FLOWER

Janet Carija Brandt

BABY BENCH

BABY BEAR

BABY CHAIR

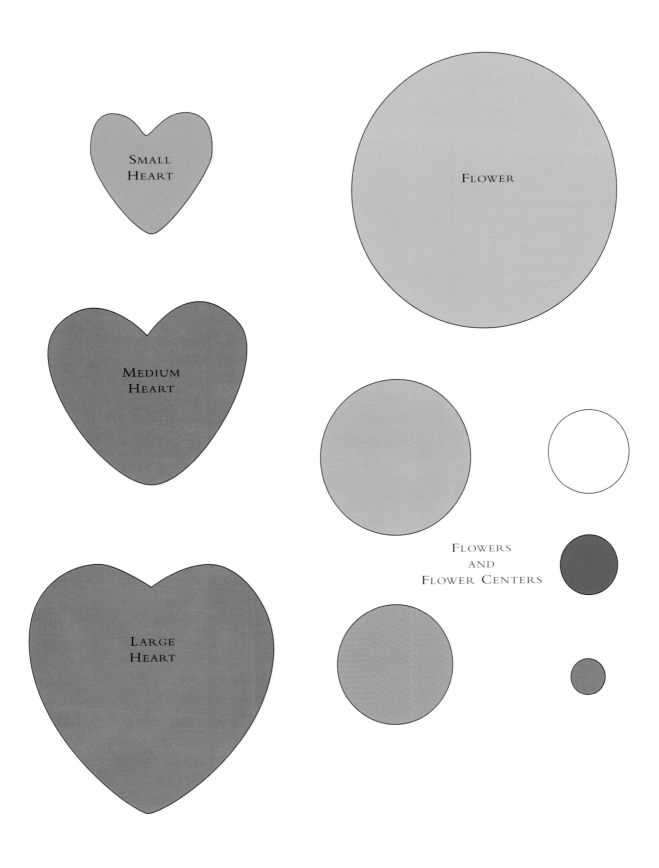

SMALL
HEART

FLOWER

MEDIUM
HEART

FLOWERS
AND
FLOWER CENTERS

LARGE
HEART

Debbie Field

WILDERNESS KIDS QUILTS

Debbie Field, producing her work through Granola Girl Designs, has emphasized her love of the outdoors in quilts, wallhangings, books, patterns, accessories, and her own fabric lines. Her work is a reflection of personal experiences since childhood— with the breathtaking sights of nature and wildlife of the great northern woods. She attributes her outdoor spirit to the warmth of her family and living an adventurous outdoor lifestyle—a tradition instilled by her parents that continues with her husband and her sons and their families.

Direct from the great outdoors, Debbie brings the wonder of the great outdoors inside with her spectacular Northwoods quilts designed for kids of all ages.

Debbie welcomes you to bear and bug country with three quilts that offer the adventurers in your life the warmth of a homemade treasure to snuggle under, to hang on the wall for lodge look décor, or to brave the cold outdoors when camping in the woods.

MATERIALS

- Light flannel fabric 1¼ yards for blocks
- Dark (rust) flannel fabric 1 yard for blocks
- Medium fabric 1 yard for sashing and inner border
- Medium-light fabric 2⅔ yards for outer border and binding
- Bear Hugs appliqué templates on pages 62–64,
- Black woodgrain-print flannel—⅝ yard for #1, #4, #11, and foot and paw claws
- Brown-fleck flannel— ⅝ yard for #2 #5, #9, #12, and #1
- Black-fleck flannel— ⅝ yard for #3, #6, #8, #10, #13, and #15
- Gray—scrap for #7 (inside eye pupil)
- Fusible web—3½ yards
- Stabilizer
- Sulky® Thread to match fabrics
- Batting—63 x 79"
- Backing fabric—3¾ yards

Finished size 57" x 73"

CUTTING

1. From Light: Cut 2— 7⅝" strips; cut strips into 6—7⅝" squares; cut each square diagonally for 12 half-square triangles.

2. Cut 3—4¼" strips; cut strips into 24—4¼" squares; cut each square diagonally for 48 half-square triangles.

3. Cut 2—3⅞" strips; cut strips into 12— 3⅞" squares.

4. From Dark: Cut 2— 7-⅝" strips; cut strips into 6—7⅝" squares; cut squares diagonally for 12 half-square triangles.

5. Cut 3—4¼" strips; cut strips into 24—4¼" squares; cut each square diagonally for 48 half-square triangles.

6. From Medium: Cut 11—2½" strips. Cut 2 strips into 8— 2½" x 10½" rectangles. Use 9 strips for the sashing and inner border.

7. From Medium-light: Cut 1—12½" strip for the top of the outer border.

8. Cut 5—9½" strips for the sides and bottom of the outer border.

9. Cut 7—3" binding strips.

Note: Cut and fuse the appliqué pieces, following the General Instructions on pages 6–7.

ASSEMBLY

1. Right sides facing, join one light and one dark 4½" half-square triangle. Press each seam toward the dark fabric. Repeat to sew 48 triangle squares for Unit A.

Unit A

2. Join two Unit A triangle squares, as shown below, to make 12 Unit B rectangles. Press each seam toward the dark fabric.

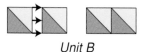

Unit B

3. Note triangle placement and join 24 triangle squares, as shown below, to make 12 Unit C rectangles. Press each seam toward the dark fabric.

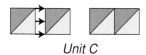

Unit C

4. Join the 3-7/8" light squares to Unit C for 12 of Unit D. Press each seam toward the square.

Unit D

5. Join 7⅝" half-square triangles for 12 Unit E triangle squares. Press seams toward dark fabric.

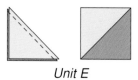

Unit E

6. Join Units B and E, noting placement, to make 12 of Unit F. Press seams toward the large triangle.

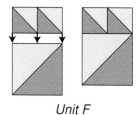

Unit F

7. Sew Unit D to the left side of Unit F, noting placement, to make 12 Bear Paws blocks. Press the seams toward Unit D.

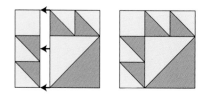

8. Sew the 2½" x 10½" medium rectangles to the blocks, as shown below, to make 4 rows of 3 blocks. Press the seams toward the sashing.

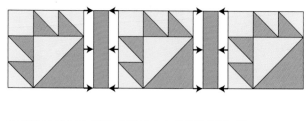

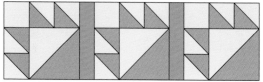

9. Measure the row width through the center for sashing length. Cut 5—2½" sashing strips to that length. Join the rows with sashing and sew a sashing strip to the bottom and top of the rows.

10. Measure the lengthwise center of the quilt for the side sashing strips. Cut 2 strips to that length and sew them to the sides. Press seams toward the sashing.

11. Measure through the center width of the quilt top for top and bottom border lengths. Cut one 12½" and one 9½" strip to length. Sew the 12½" strip to the top and the 9½" strip to the bottom of the quilt. Press the seams toward the borders.

12. Measure through the center length of the quilt top and cut 2 outer border strips to that length. Sew the borders to the quilt top and press the seams toward the borders.

13. Refer to the illustration, below, for placement and General Instructions, pages 6–7, to cut, fuse, stabilize, and appliqué the pattern pieces.

14. Layer backing, batting, and the quilt top. Baste the layers and hand- or machine-quilt as desired. Finish the quilt by sewing on the binding, following the steps in the General Instructions, pages 6–7.

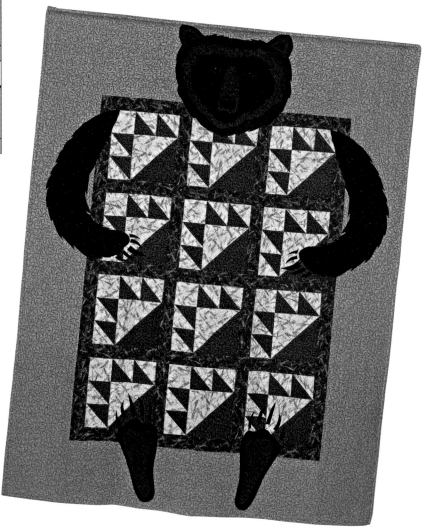

Finished size 44" x 65"

MATERIALS

- Light solid fabric ½ yard for appliqué blocks and top panel

- Light print fabric ¾ yard for blocks

- Dark green print fabric ⅓ yard for blocks

- Medium green print fabric 2 yards for blocks, outer border, and binding

- Black background print ½ yard for sashing and inner borders

- Don't Bug Me appliqué templates on pages 104–111 and the following assorted fabrics: Black—for caterpillar head, dragonfly, ants, mosquito, beetle, eyes

- Blue plaid—⅓ yard for letters

- Brown—caterpillar, grasshopper, dragonfly wings, beetle, mosquito

- Brown/black—spiders

- Green—praying mantis, grasshopper, caterpillar, and millipede

- Woodgrain-print—spiders, mosquito wings

- Fusible web—1¾ yards

- Stabilizer

- Sulky® Thread to match fabrics

- Backing fabric—3 yards

- Batting—50" x 72"

CUTTING

1. From Light solid: Cut 1—8½" x 30½" strip.

2. Cut 1—6½" strip; cut the strip into 6—6½" squares.

4. From Light print: Cut 10—2½" strips.

5. From Dark green: Cut 4—2½" strips.

6. From Medium green: Cut 5—5½" strips for the outer border.

7. Cut 6—2¾" strips for binding.

8. Cut 4—2½" strips for blocks.

9. From Black background print: Cut 6—2" strips for sashing and inner border.

ASSEMBLY

1. Sew a dark green strip to each side of a light print strip. Repeat to make a second strip set. Press the seams toward the dark fabric. Cut the strip sets into 24—2½" x 6½" segments.

24—2-1/2x6-1/2"

2. Sew a light print strip to each side of a medium green strip. Repeat to make four strip sets. Press the seams toward the medium fabric. Cut the strips into 17—6½" squares for Rail Blocks and 12—2½" x 6½" segments that will be used to make Nine-Patch Blocks.

12—2-1/2x6-1/2"

12—2-1/2x6-1/2"
Rail Blocks

3. Assemble two dark-light-dark segments and one light-medium-light segment to make 12 Nine-Patch Blocks, shown below. Press the seams in one direction.

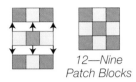

12—Nine Patch Blocks

4. Join the Nine-Patch Blocks with the Rail Blocks to form Rows 1, 3, 5, and 7, shown below. Press the seams toward the Rail Blocks.

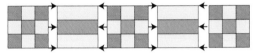

Rows 1, 3, 5, and 7

Join the remaining Rail Blocks with the solid 6½" squares to form Rows 2, 4, and 6, shown below. Press the seams toward the Rail Blocks.

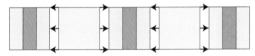

Rows 2, 4, and 6

5. Join the rows as shown in the Finished Quilt Assembly, right.
6. Refer to the Finished Quilt Assembly, right, for placement and the General Instructions, pages 6–7, to fuse, cut out, position, and appliqué the blocks and the 8½" x 30" rectangle. Use a small zigzag stitch and matching or coordinating threads to appliqué each piece in place.

NOTE: *Dashed lines outside bug templates indicate stitching lines for details.*

7. Sew a 30½" sashing strip to the lower edge of the Don't Bug Me rectangle. Sew the joined piece to the block assembly. Press the seams toward the sashing strip.

8. Measure the quilt width along the center and cut two inner border strips to that length. Sew one strip to the top and one to the bottom of the quilt top. Measure the quilt top lengthwise through the center and cut two strips to that measurement. Sew one strip to each side of the quilt. Press the seams toward the borders.
9. Measure the quilt top widthwise through the center. Cut two outer border strips to length. Sew one to the top and one to the bottom of the quilt. Press the seams toward the borders. Measure the length of the quilt top, cut two outer border strips, and sew them to the sides of the quilt. Press seams toward the borders.
10. Layer the backing fabric, batting, and quilt top. Baste the layers together and quilt by hand or machine as desired. Finish the quilt by sewing on the binding, following the steps in the General Instructions on pages 6–7.

Finished size 56" x 68"

MATERIALS

- Light print fabric—2 yards for background

- Green fabric—1 yard for trees

- Brown fabric—¼ yard for tree trunks

- Rust on navy leaf-print fabric—¾ yard for sashing and inner border

- Rust small muted-print fabric—1⅝ yard for outer border and binding

- Fusible web—3½ yards

- Stabilizer

- Sulky® Thread to match fabrics

- Backing—3½ yards; Batting—62" x 74"

Woodland ABCs templates on pages 55-65, Fishing Tales turtle on page 61, and the following assorted fabrics:

- Black—5 x 7" for bear body, 4 x 6" for loon; 3 x 6" for skunk; small pieces for caterpillar belly, goose neck; black-and-white multicolor for loon wing

- Blue—water for fish, water for loon

- Bright green—caterpillar body

- Brown—⅓ yard for alphabet, 5" square for moose body, 3 x 9" for turtle body and head; small pieces for bear nose, eagle beak and wings

- Dark Brown—5" square for vole, 3 x 5" for otter, 4 x 5" for moose head, 4 x 8" for porcupine, 6 x 7" for nest; small pieces for deer antlers, goose wing

- Ecru or off-white—skunk back and tail, eagle head and tail, raccoon mask

- Gray-black print—6 x 7" for raccoon

- Gray-brown—7 x 8" for wolf

- Gray-blue print—nest eggs

- Green—3 x 6" print for turtle shell; vole grass

- Light Brown—4 x 6" for deer body, 6" square for vole ground; small pieces for nest, goose body and throat, otter chest and legs

- Multicolor print—5 x 6" for fish

- White—for deer chest, loon neck and chest,

- Woodgrain-print—moose antlers

CUTTING

1. From Light: Cut 3—10½" strips; cut the strips into 10—10½" squares and 2—8½" x 10½" rectangles for the appliqué blocks.

2. Cut 2—2⅞" strips; cut each strip into 26—2⅞" squares. Diagonally cut each square for 52 Unit F half-square triangles.

3. Cut 10—2½" strips.

4. Cut 4 strips into 26—2½" x 4½" Unit B rectangles.

5. Cut 3 strips into 26—2½" x 3½" Unit E rectangles.

6. Cut 3 strips into 26—2½" x 4" Unit I rectangles.

7. From Green: Cut 2—2⅞" strips; cut each strip into 26—2⅞" squares. Diagonally cut each square for 52 Unit D half-square triangles.

8. Cut 9—2½" strips;

9. Cut 1 strip into 13—2½" Unit C squares.

10. Cut 4 strips into 52—2½" Unit A squares.

11. Cut 4 strips into 26—2½" x 4½" Unit G rectangles.

12. From Brown: Cut 1—2½" strip; cut the strip into 13—1½" x 2½" Unit H rectangles.

13. From Rust on navy leaf-print: Cut 10—2½" strips for sashing and inner border.

14. From Rust small muted-print: Cut 7—4½" strips for the outer border.

15. Cut 6—3" strips for binding.

Note: Cut and fuse the appliqué pieces, following the General Instructions on pages 6–7.

BLOCK ASSEMBLY

1. Mark a diagonal line along the wrong side of each of the 52 Unit A 2½" green squares.

2. Using 26 Unit A squares and 26 Unit B rectangles, position Unit A facedown on Unit B, noting placement, below. Sew along the diagonal line to make 13 left units and 13 right units. Trim the seam to ¼" and press each seam toward the dark fabric.

13 left units   *13 right units*

3. Join a left and right unit to make a tree top unit (Row 1, below) for 13 tree top units. Press the seams in the same direction.

  *Row 1*

4. Using 26 Unit A squares and 26 Unit E rectangles, place Unit A facedown on Unit E, noting placement, below. Sew along the diagonal line to make 13 left units and 13 right units. Trim the seam to ¼" and press each seam toward the dark fabric.

13 left units   *13 right units*

5. Sew a left and right unit to opposite sides of Unit C to make Row 2, below. Press seams to the center.

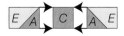 *Row 2*

6. Right sides facing, join a Unit D and Unit F half-square triangle to make 26 left and 26 right end units, below. Press seams toward the dark fabric.

*26 left
end units*   *26 right
end units*

7. Sew each left and right unit to opposite sides of a Unit G rectangle to make 26 units for Rows 3 and 4, below. Press the seams toward the center.

    Rows 3 and 4

8. Sew a Unit I large rectangle to opposite sides of a Unit H small rectangle to make 13 Row 5 tree trunk units. Press the seams toward the center.

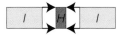  *Row 5*

9. Layout and join Rows 1-5 to make 13 Pine Tree blocks. Press the seams toward the top of the tree. Set the blocks aside.

10. Layout, but DO NOT JOIN, the Pine Tree blocks and the Appliqué blocks, referring to the Finished Quilt Assembly on page 49, and using the 8½" x 10½" rectangles at the centers of Rows 2 and 4.

11. Refer to Finished Quilt Assembly, page 56, and General Instructions, pages 6-7, to fuse, position, and appliqué. Use a small zigzag stitch and matching thread. If the appliqué blocks distort from stitching, press and shape to size.

12. Sew the Pine Tree and completed Appliqué blocks together in 5 rows of 5 blocks each. The rows should measure approximately 44½" wide.

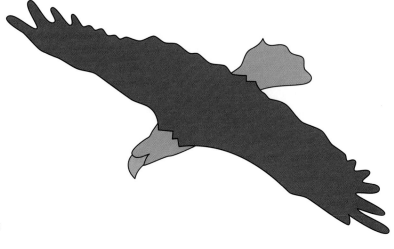

13. Join the sashing and inner border strips for a continuous length. Measure the width of Row 1 through the center. Cut two lengths to that measurement and sew one to each long edge of the row. Measure Rows 2, 3, 4, and 5; cut and sew a strip to the lower long edge only of each row. Join the rows and sashing strips. Press the seams toward the strips.

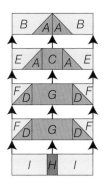
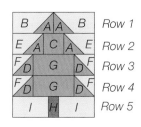

14. Measure the length of the quilt top through the center. Cut two inner border strips to that length and sew one to each side of the quilt. Press the seams toward the borders.

15. Join the outer border strips for a continuous length. Measure the length of the quilt top through the center. Cut two strips to that length and sew one to each side of the quilt top. Press the seams toward the borders. Measure the width of the quilt top through the center and cut two strips to that length. Sew one strip to the top and one strip to the bottom of the quilt. Press the seams toward the borders.

16. Layer the backing fabric, batting, and quilt top. Baste the layers together and quilt by hand or machine as desired. Finish the quilt by sewing on the binding, following the steps in the General Instructions, pages 6–7.

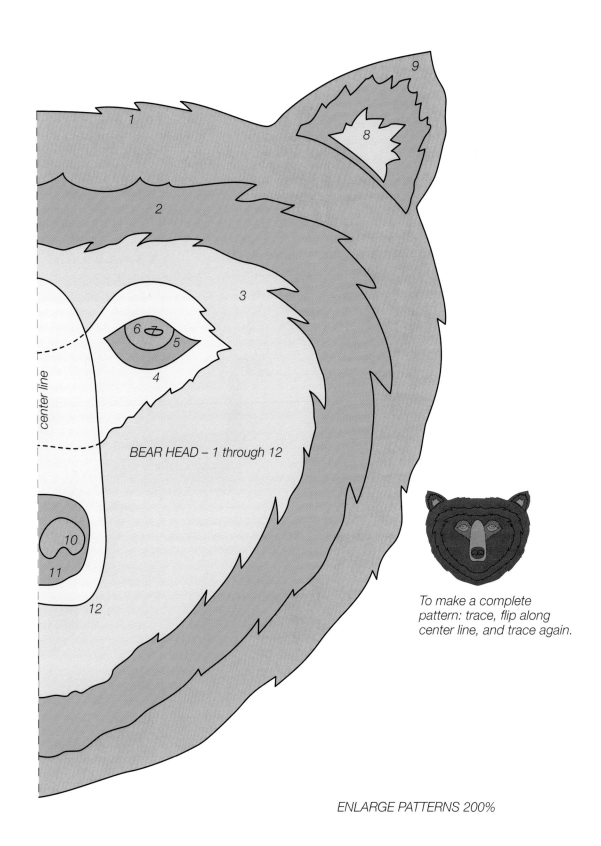

1

9

2

8

3

6 7

5

center line

4

BEAR HEAD – 1 through 12

10

11

12

To make a complete
pattern: trace, flip along
center line, and trace again.

ENLARGE PATTERNS 200%

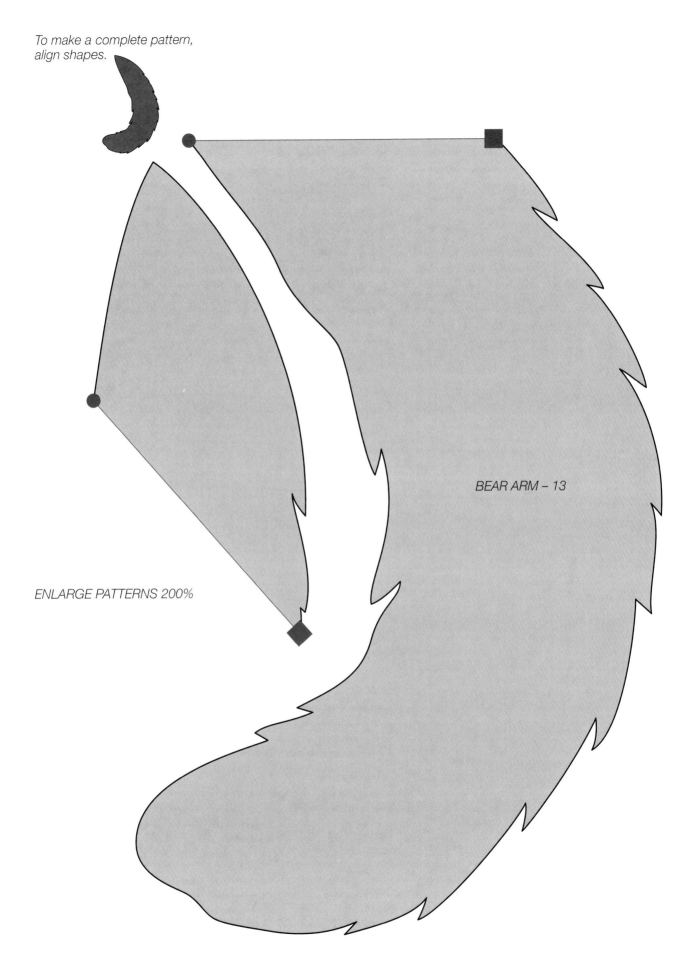

To make a complete pattern, align shapes.

ENLARGE PATTERNS 200%

BEAR ARM – 13

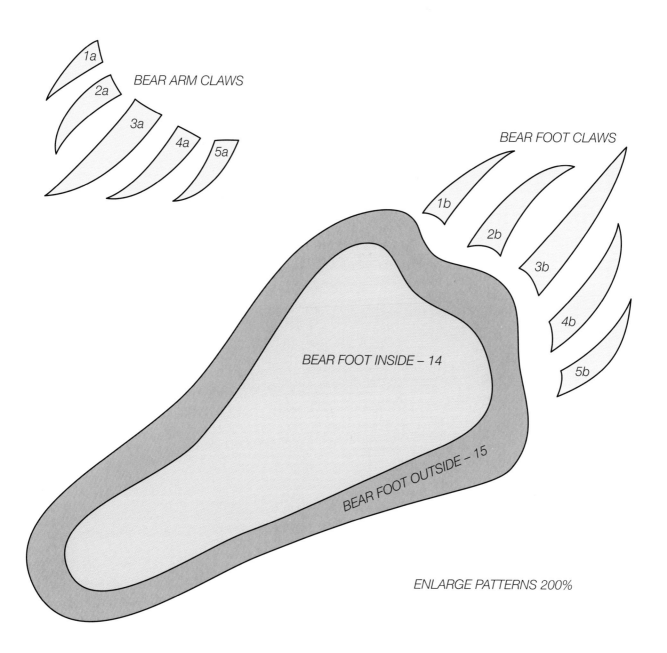

BEAR ARM CLAWS

1a

2a

3a

4a

5a

BEAR FOOT CLAWS

1b

2b

3b

4b

5b

BEAR FOOT INSIDE – 14

BEAR FOOT OUTSIDE – 15

ENLARGE PATTERNS 200%

ALPHABET LETTERS
– ABCDEFG

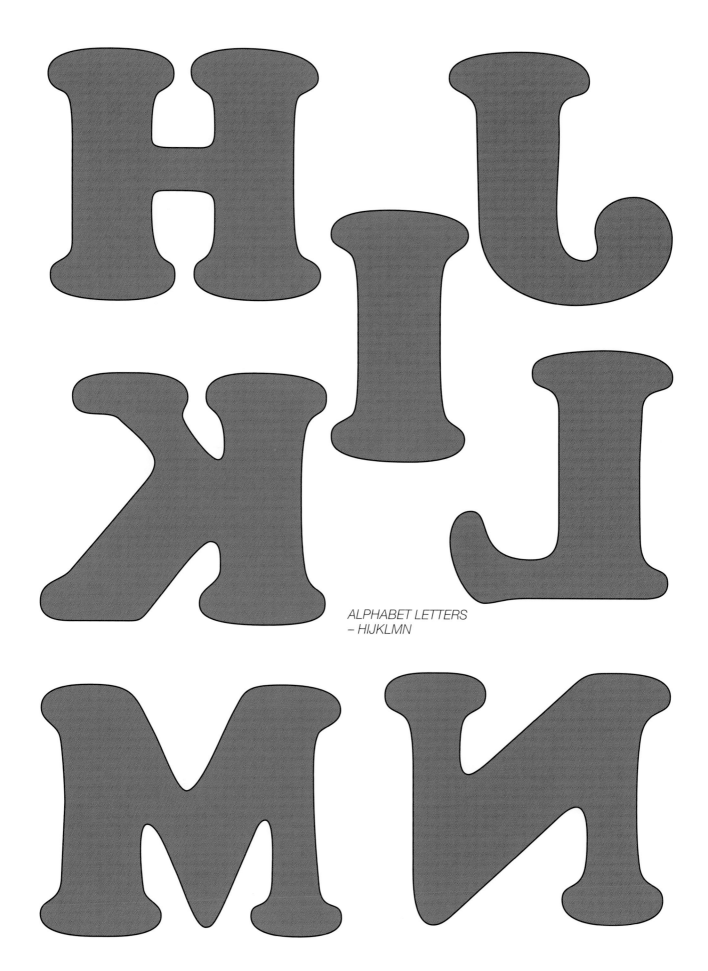

ALPHABET LETTERS
– HIJKLMN

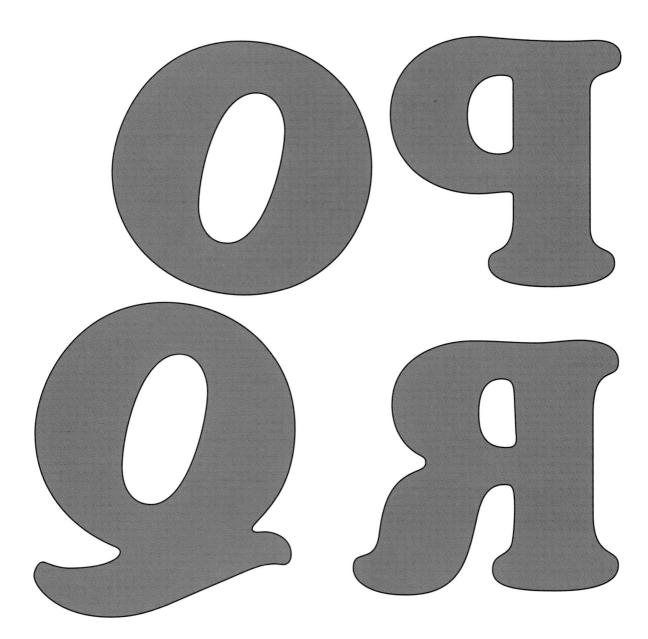

*ALPHABET LETTERS
– OPQRST*

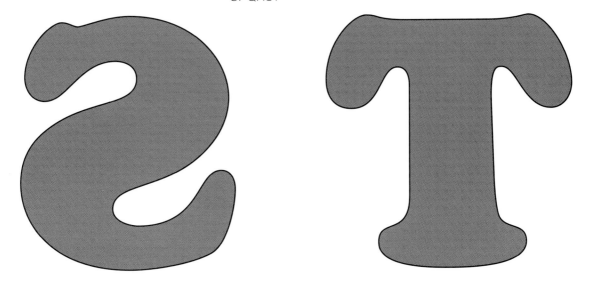

ALPHABET LETTERS
– UVWXYZ

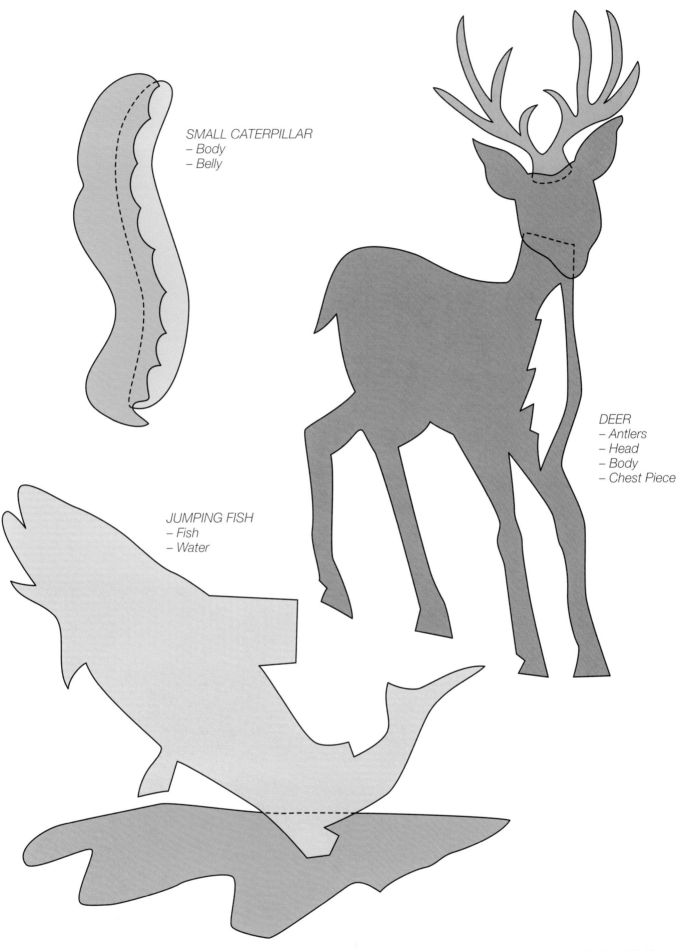

SMALL CATERPILLAR
– Body
– Belly

DEER
– Antlers
– Head
– Body
– Chest Piece

JUMPING FISH
– Fish
– Water

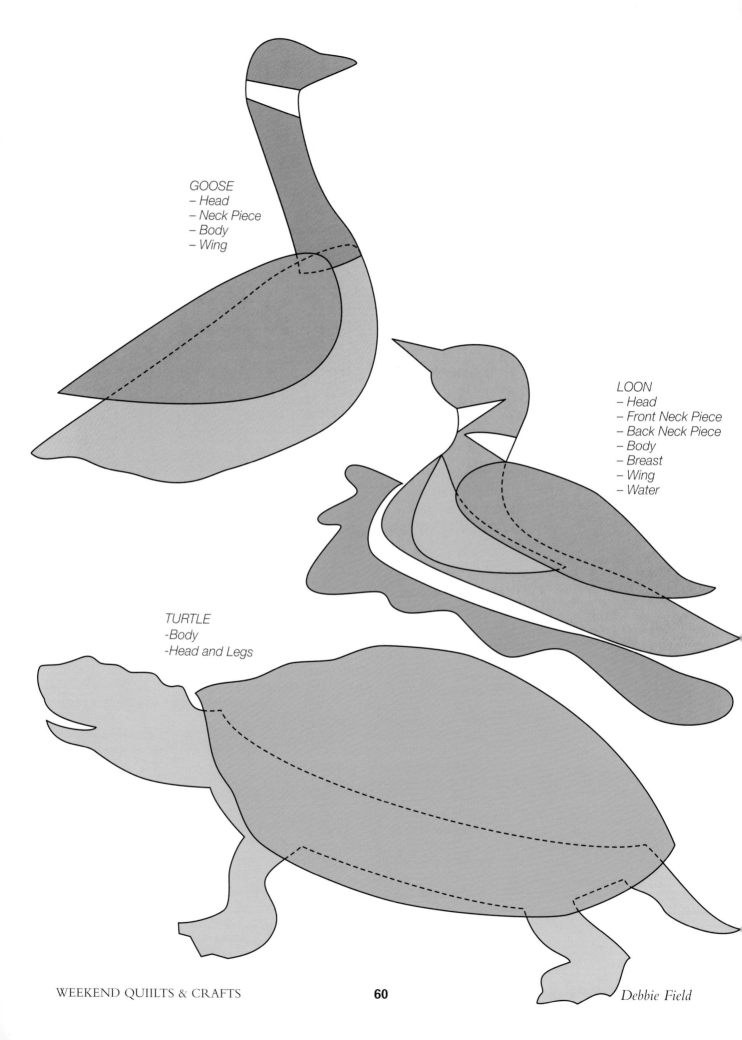

GOOSE
– Head
– Neck Piece
– Body
– Wing

LOON
– Head
– Front Neck Piece
– Back Neck Piece
– Body
– Breast
– Wing
– Water

TURTLE
-Body
-Head and Legs

WEEKEND QUIILTS & CRAFTS

Debbie Field

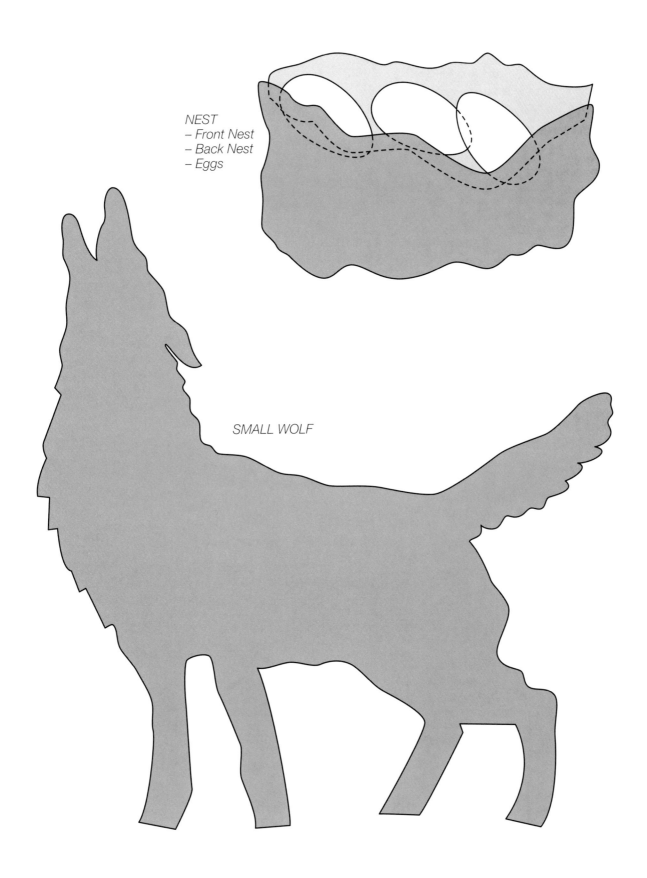

NEST
– Front Nest
– Back Nest
– Eggs

SMALL WOLF

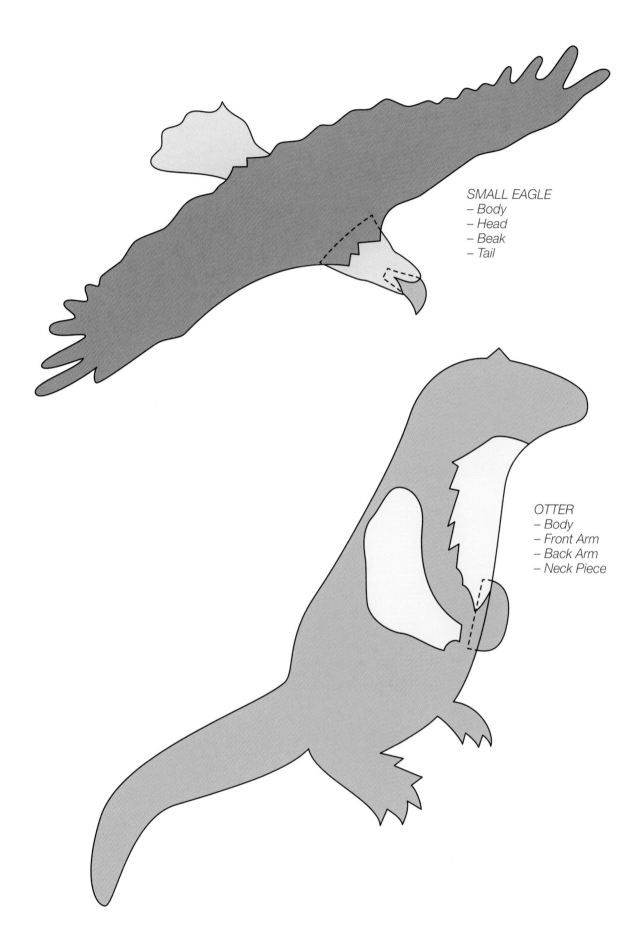

SMALL EAGLE
– Body
– Head
– Beak
– Tail

OTTER
– Body
– Front Arm
– Back Arm
– Neck Piece

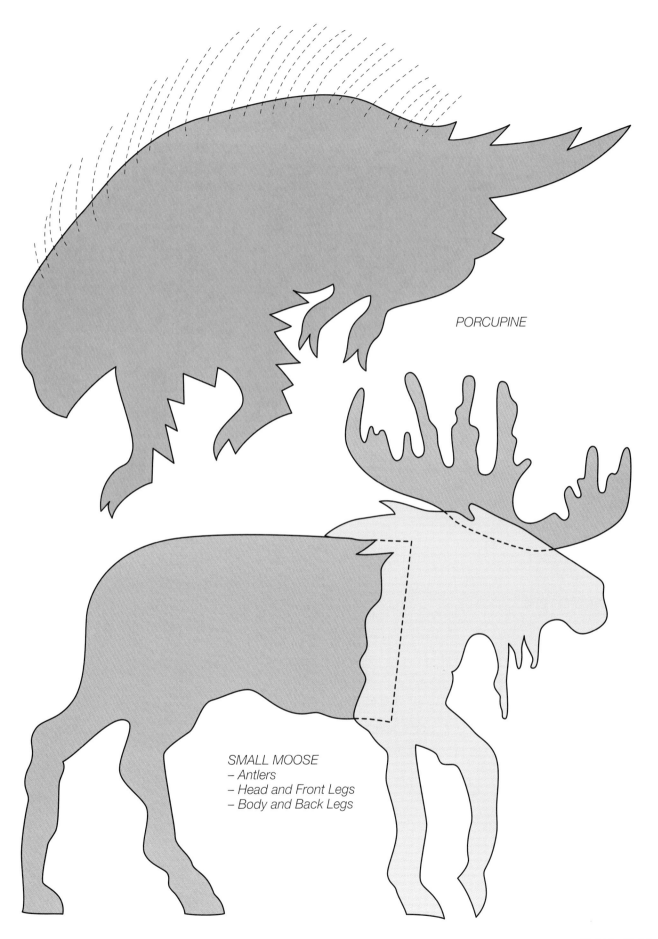

PORCUPINE

SMALL MOOSE
– Antlers
– Head and Front Legs
– Body and Back Legs

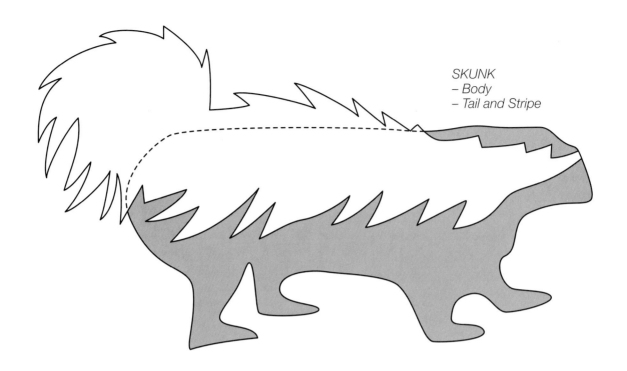

SKUNK
– Body
– Tail and Stripe

SMALL BEAR
– Body
– Nose

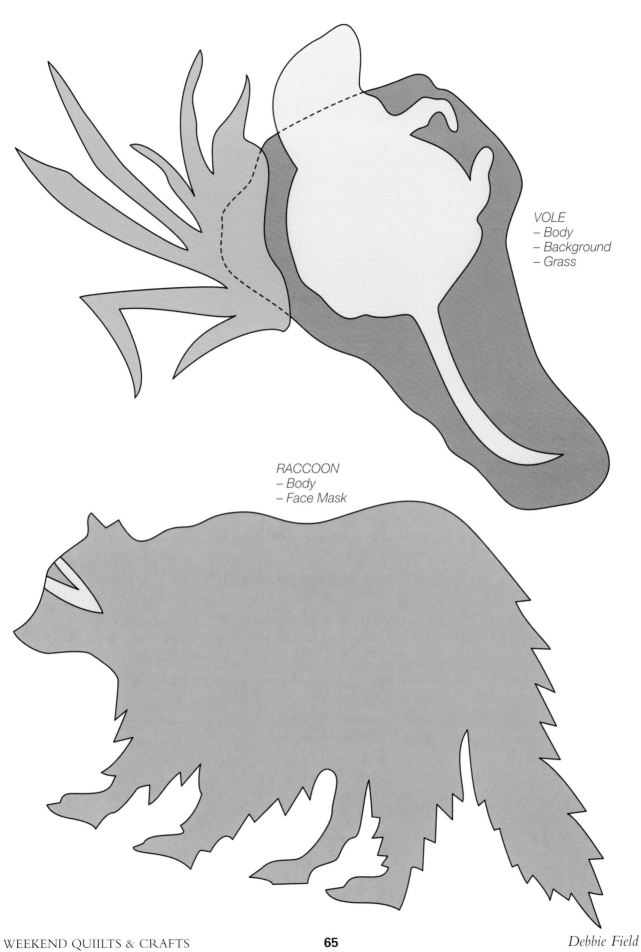

VOLE
– Body
– Background
– Grass

RACCOON
– Body
– Face Mask

LETTERING – DON'T

ANT

LETTERING – BUG ME

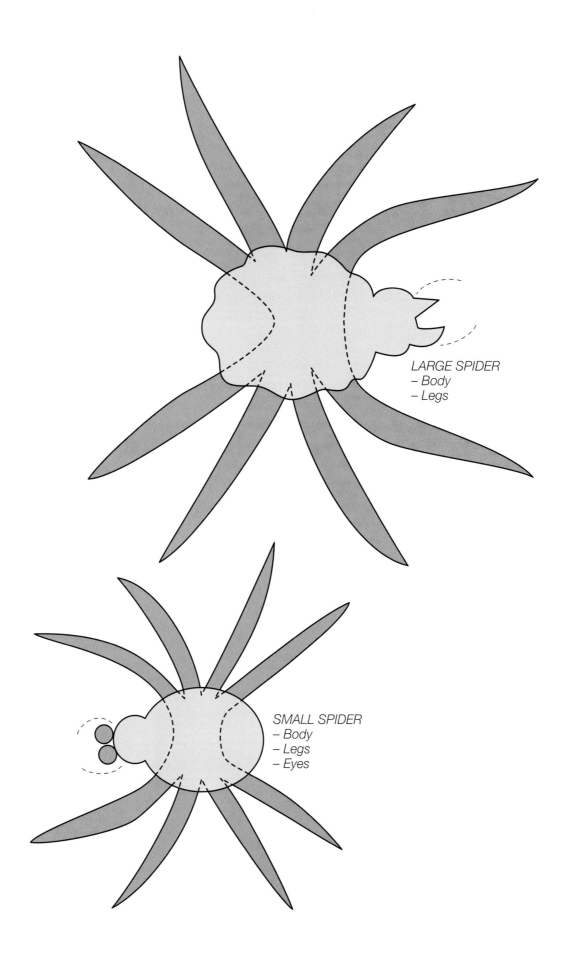

LARGE SPIDER
– Body
– Legs

SMALL SPIDER
– Body
– Legs
– Eyes

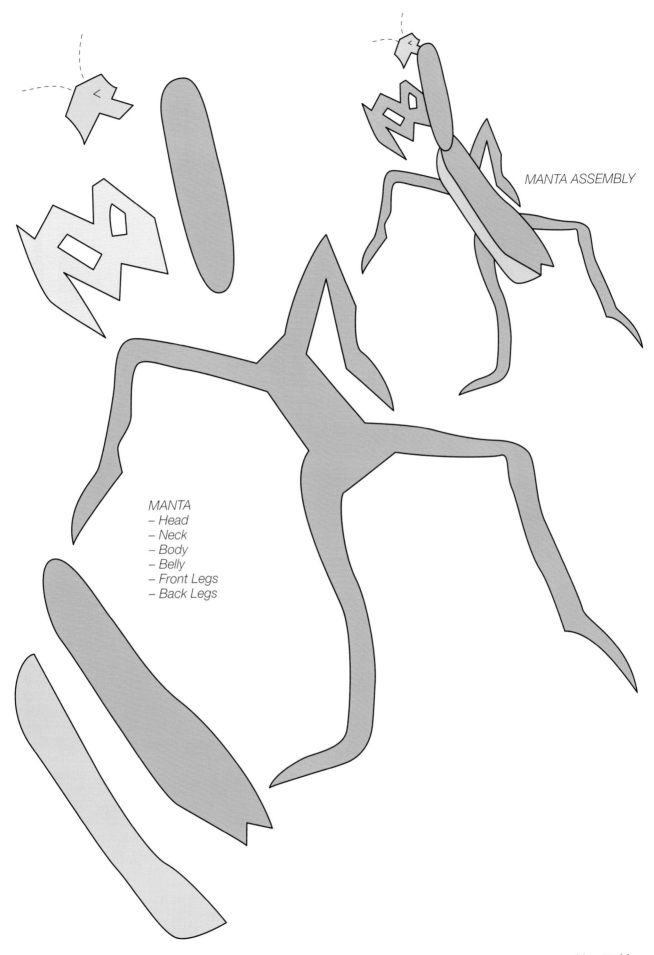

MANTA ASSEMBLY

MANTA
– Head
– Neck
– Body
– Belly
– Front Legs
– Back Legs

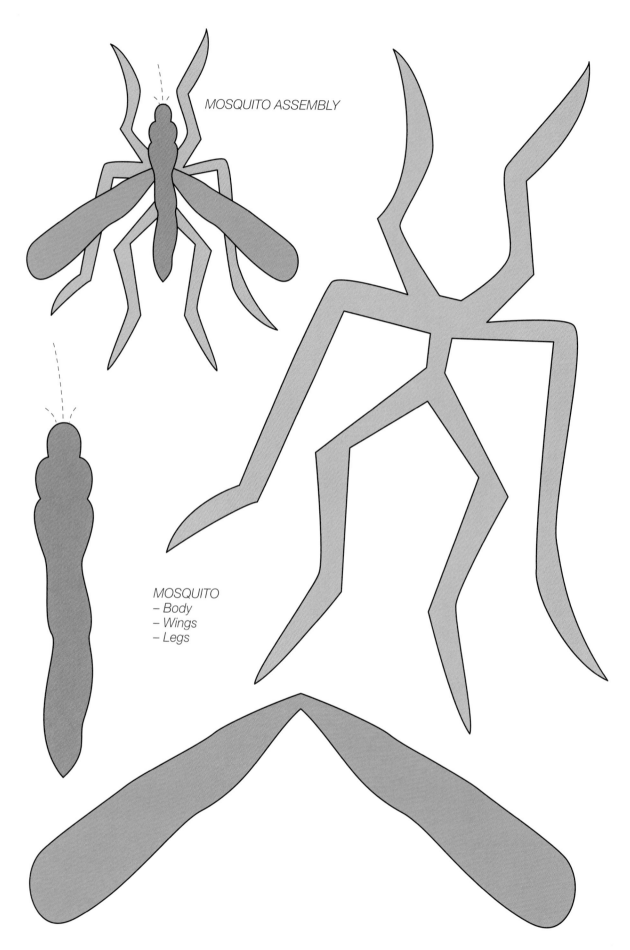

MOSQUITO ASSEMBLY

MOSQUITO
– Body
– Wings
– Legs

Debbie Field

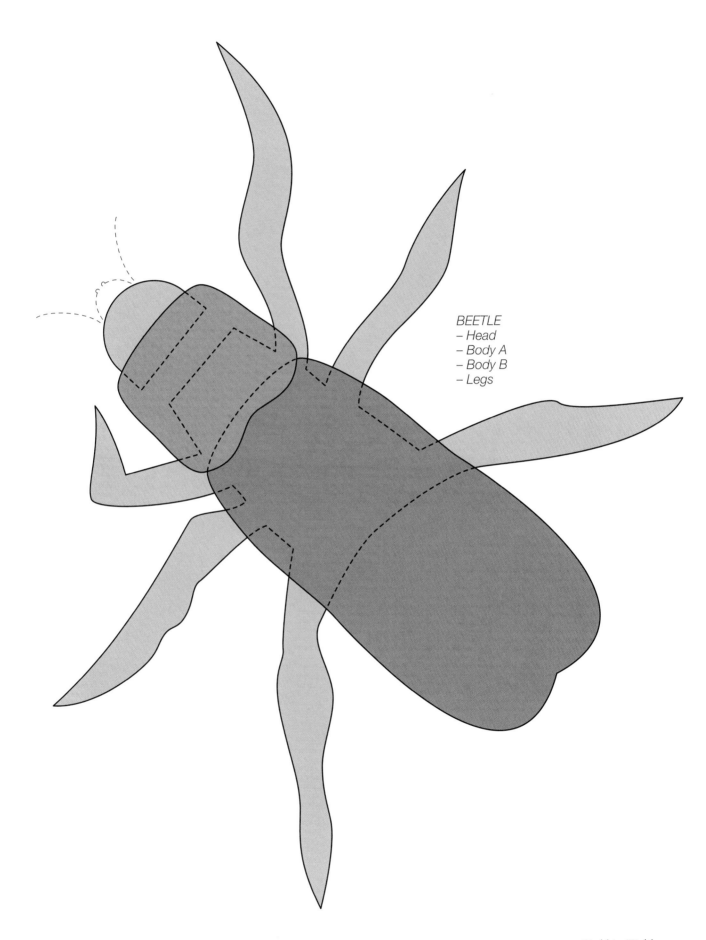

BEETLE
– Head
– Body A
– Body B
– Legs

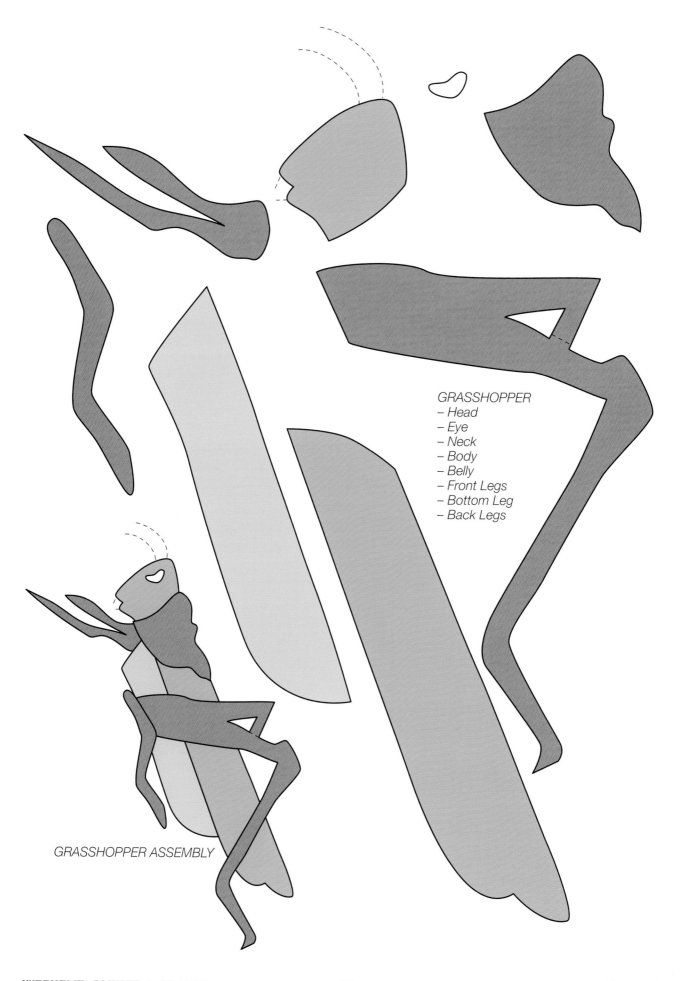

GRASSHOPPER
– Head
– Eye
– Neck
– Body
– Belly
– Front Legs
– Bottom Leg
– Back Legs

GRASSHOPPER ASSEMBLY

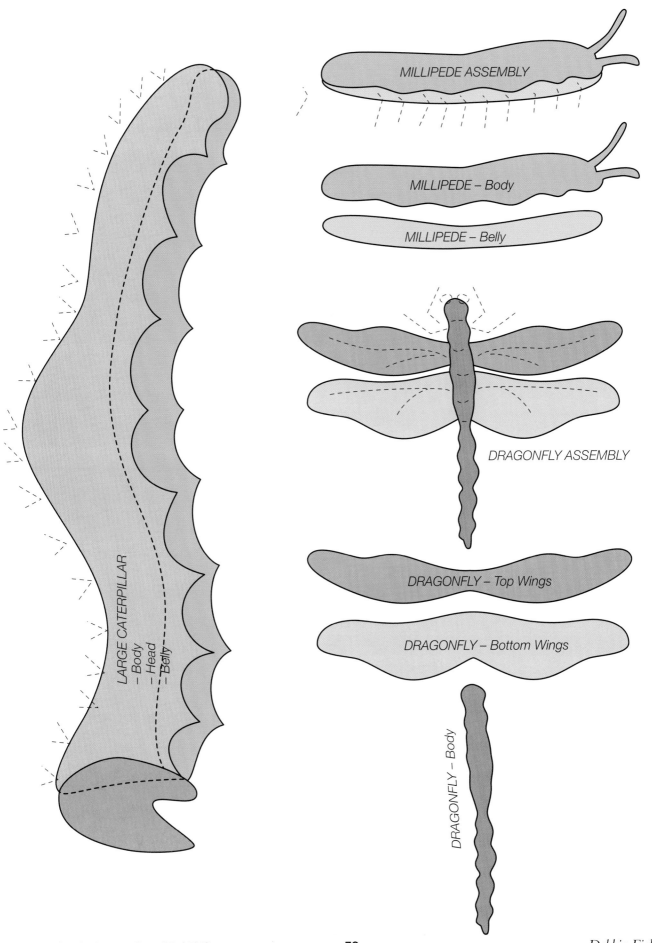

MILLIPEDE ASSEMBLY

MILLIPEDE – Body

MILLIPEDE – Belly

DRAGONFLY ASSEMBLY

DRAGONFLY – Top Wings

DRAGONFLY – Bottom Wings

DRAGONFLY – Body

LARGE CATERPILLAR
– Body
– Head
– Belly

McKenna Ryan

CATCHING MEMORIES

Father's Day holds special meaning for McKenna Ryan, whose father passed away when she was still a teenager. He was a man of many talents—a master violinist, a pilot, and a fisherman, among other things—and her memory of him continues to inspire McKenna today. "He was such a creative soul," she says. "And I know he would be so proud if he could see what I'm doing now."

What she's doing now is running a business called Pine Needles, creating and marketing a line of original quilt designs inspired by the Northwoods.

But McKenna inherited more than creativity from her father. She, too, loves fishing and the outdoors, and those two passions inspired her to create this wonderful collection for Father's Day or a special birthday. The wallhanging features a father and his child enjoying a special time together. (McKenna designed the figures in silhouette so that the child could represent either a boy or a girl!) Unique accents such as the three-dimensional fishing line and the real lure add special touches to this fun quilt. Coordinating photo frames and lamp trims bring the outdoors inside, making Dad's den a great place to plan his next fishing trip (or dream about the one that got away!).

MATERIALS

- ■ ⅓ yard each of two medium brown print fabrics for background
- ■ ⅓ yard of light tan print fabric for inner border
- ■ ⅝ yard of green-and-brown leaf print fabric for outer border
- ■ ½ yard of black fabric for appliqués and binding
- ■ Large scraps of assorted green, blue, purple, and dark brown fabrics for appliqués
- ■ 1 yard of fabric for backing
- ■ 29" x 36" piece of batting
- ■ Fusible web
- ■ Clear nylon thread
- ■ Variegated thread
- ■ Black and cream embroidery floss
- ■ One small doll eye
- ■ One fly lure
- ■ White craft glue

Quick-Sew Wallhanging

Finished size 27" x 34"

CUTTING

1. From one medium brown print background fabric, cut a 9" x 25½" rectangle for the sky. From the other background fabric, cut a 7½" x 25½" rectangle for the lake.

2. From the light tan print border fabric, cut two 2¾" x 25½" strips and two 1½" x 20½" strips.

3. From the leaf print fabric, cut four 4" x 27½" strips.

4. From the backing fabric, cut a 29" x 36" rectangle.

5. From the black fabric, cut four 2½" binding strips across the width of the fabric.

6. Refer to the General Instructions on page 6 to trace, apply fusible web to, and cut out the following appliqué pieces from the patterns on pages 78-85: One each of trees A, B (connect both patterns), C, and D, large island and its reflection, grass, boats A and B, child, man and fishing pole, boat reflection, small island and its reflection, medium fish, and bird B. Cut two of bird A.

PIECING AND ASSEMBLY

1. Referring to Diagram A, assemble the top as follows: Sew the two background pieces together to make a 16" x 25½" rectangle. Sew the 2¾"-wide light tan strips to the top and bottom of the rectangle; press the seam allowances toward the strips. Sew the 1½"-wide light tan strips to the sides, press. Sew a 4"-wide leaf print strip to the top and bottom of the rectangle; press. Sew the remaining 4"-wide strips to the sides, and press.

2. Referring to the photograph, and following the directions below, fuse the appliqué pieces to the background, layering as indicated by the dashed lines on the patterns. For best results, position all pieces and check placement before fusing; adjust as needed.

3. Position the small island and its reflection at the seam between the sky and the lake; fuse. Position the four trees, slipping B under A and C under B as marked on the patterns; fuse. Position and fuse the large island, slightly overlapping the bottoms of the trees. Fuse the grass to the lower edge of the island. Position and fuse the island's reflection.

4. Position the two boat pieces and the silhouettes; fuse. Add the reflection.

5. Fuse the medium fish at the lower right and the birds at the upper right.

FINISHING

1. Referring to the General Instructions on page 7, layer the wallhanging.

2. Using clear nylon thread, stitch just inside the edge of all appliqué pieces. Using variegated rayon thread, machine-quilt a casual wavy pattern in the bottom half of the background and light tan border and freeform cloud shapes in the top half.

3. Use clear nylon thread to quilt a loose meandering pattern in the outer border.

4. Trim the edges of the layers even. Prepare the binding strips and a hanging sleeve as directed in the General Instructions on page 7; pin to the back.

5. Referring to the General Instructions on page 7 for mitered corners, sew the binding in place; fold and whipstitch to the back.

6. To make the child's fishing rod, thread a needle with a 6-inch piece of black floss and knot the end. Bring the floss to the front of the wallhanging at the end of the child's arms. Five inches away, push the needle back through the quilt; pull the floss taut enough so it doesn't sag; knot the floss.

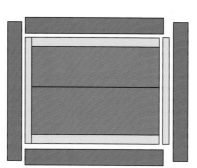

DIAGRAM A

7. To make the child's fishing line, thread a needle with a 7" piece of cream embroidery floss and knot the end. Bring the floss to the front of the wallhanging at the end of the child's rod, and take it through to the back about 4 inches away, leaving a slack line of floss on the front. To shape the line, put a little white craft glue between thumb and forefinger, and run along the length of the floss. Shape as desired, and allow to dry. The line will become slightly stiff and will hold its shape.

8. To make the man's line, thread a needle with a 14" piece of cream embroidery floss and knot the end. Bring it to the front of the wallhanging at the end of the rod, and take it to the back near the fish's mouth. Use a pair of needle-nose pliers to pinch the barb off a lure; stitch the lure in place at the end of the floss, burying the tip inside the batting. Sew a doll's eye to the fish.

Rod and Reel Photo Frame

8½" x 10" (image size 4" x 6")

MATERIALS

- Scraps of dark brown, light brown, and black fabric
- Scraps of felt to match fabrics
- Fusible web
- Clear nylon thread
- Variegated thread
- Black embroidery floss
- Fly lure
- 8½" x 10" wood frame
- Hot-glue gun and glue sticks

DIAGRAM B

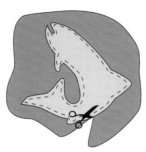

DIAGRAM C

CUTTING

1. Refer to the General Instructions on page 6 to trace, apply fusible web to, and cut out the following appliqué pieces on pages 81 and 85: Medium fish; rod parts A, B, C, and D; and reel.

ASSEMBLY

1. Fuse the medium fish to a slightly larger piece of felt in a matching color. See Diagram B.

2. Using clear nylon thread, stitch just inside the edge of the fish. Using variegated thread, add decorative stitching to accent the fins and tail. Stitch a round eye.

3. Trim the felt along the edge of the pattern piece as shown in Diagram C. Hot-glue the fish to the frame.

4. Fuse the rod parts and the reel to a piece of black felt, overlapping as indicated by the dashed pattern lines. Using clear nylon thread, stitch just inside the edges of the pattern pieces.

5. Trim the felt, and hot-glue the rod and reel to the frame. Fold over ¼" at the end of the rod, and hold in place with a dot of glue. Thread a 14" piece

of black embroidery floss through the loop. Glue one end of the floss under the edge of the reel, and glue the other end near the mouth of the fish.

6. Using needle-nose pliers, pinch the barb off a fly lure. Hot-glue the lure to the frame, covering the end of the floss.

Bear Photo Frame

7½" x 9½" (image size 3" x 5")

MATERIALS

- Scraps of light brown, dark brown, and green fabrics
- Scraps of felt to match fabrics
- Fusible web
- Clear nylon thread
- Variegated thread
- 7½" x 9½" wood frame
- Hot-glue gun and glue sticks

CUTTING

1. Refer to the General Instructions on page 6 to trace, apply fusible web to, and cut out the following appliqué pieces on pages 78-85: Bear, small fish, tree A, and trunk.

ASSEMBLY

1. Peel the paper backing off the fish, and place the fish inside the bear's mouth. Fuse the pieces as a unit to a slightly larger piece of felt. Fuse the tree and trunk to a piece of felt.

2. Using clear nylon thread, stitch just inside the edge of the pattern pieces. Trim the felt close to the pattern pieces; hot-glue to the frame.

Lamp Trims

MATERIALS

- Scraps of green, brown, and black fabrics
- Fusible web
- Scraps of black felt
- Lamp with 10" shade★
- Clear nylon thread
- Variegated thread

★Note: The lampshade shown was purchased with the leather lacing already on it. Add lacing to your shade, if desired, using a ¼" single-hole punch and 1/16" leather strips.

CUTTING

1. Refer to the General Instructions on page 6 to trace, apply fusible web to, and cut out the following appliqué pieces on pages 84-85: Large fish, and fly lure pieces A, B, C, D, E, F, and G.

ASSEMBLY

1. To make the lampshade trim, fuse the fish pieces to a slightly larger piece of black felt, overlapping the pieces as indicated by the dashed lines on the fish pattern.

2. Using clear nylon thread, stitch just inside the edges of the appliqué pieces. Fuse the felt to a piece of fusible web. Trim the felt close to the edges of the pattern piece. Carefully fuse the fish to the lampshade.

3. To make the lamp-base trim, layer the lure pieces in order on a slightly larger piece of black felt, overlapping as indicated by the dashed lines on the patterns; fuse.

4. Using clear nylon thread, stitch just inside the edge of the appliqué pieces. Using variegated thread, add decorative stitching as shown in the photograph. Trim away the background felt.

5. Attach the lure to post of the lamp base with a small dot of hot glue or a piece of double-sided foam tape.

JOURNAL COVER

Make a special place for Dad to record memorable trips and favorite fishing holes. Start with a blank journal with a plain cover. Cover the journal with an attractive brown paper; handmade paper is especially nice. Then, using the same technique used for the fish on the photo frame, make a medium fish, but trace the pattern in reverse. Glue the fish to cover. Use needle-nose pliers to pinch the barbs off two fly lures; glue them to the cover. If you prefer, cover and decorate an address book instead.

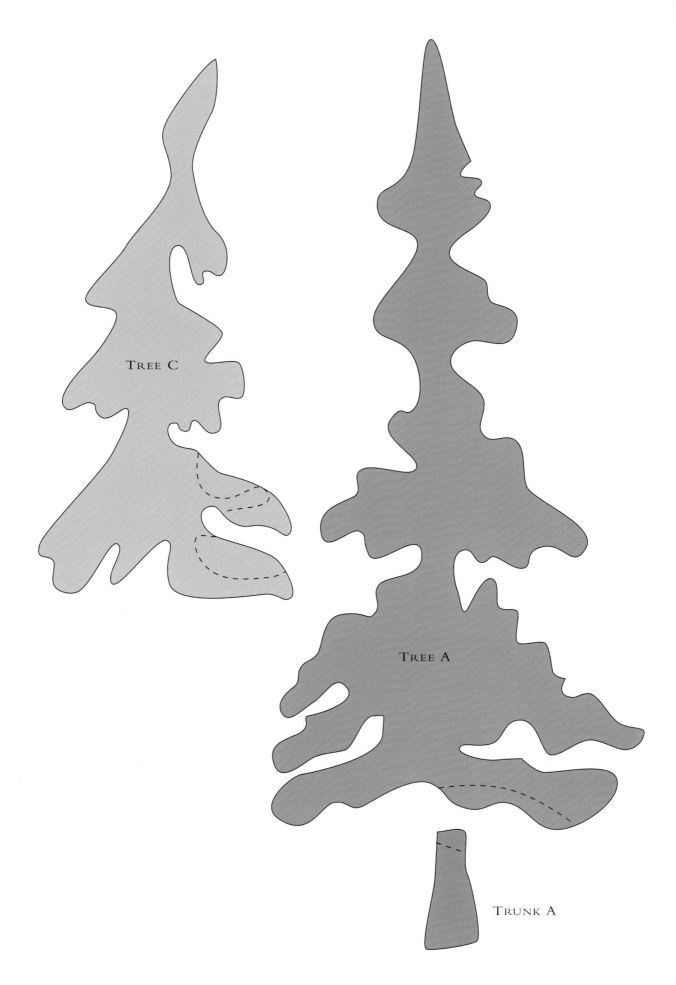

TREE C

TREE A

TRUNK A

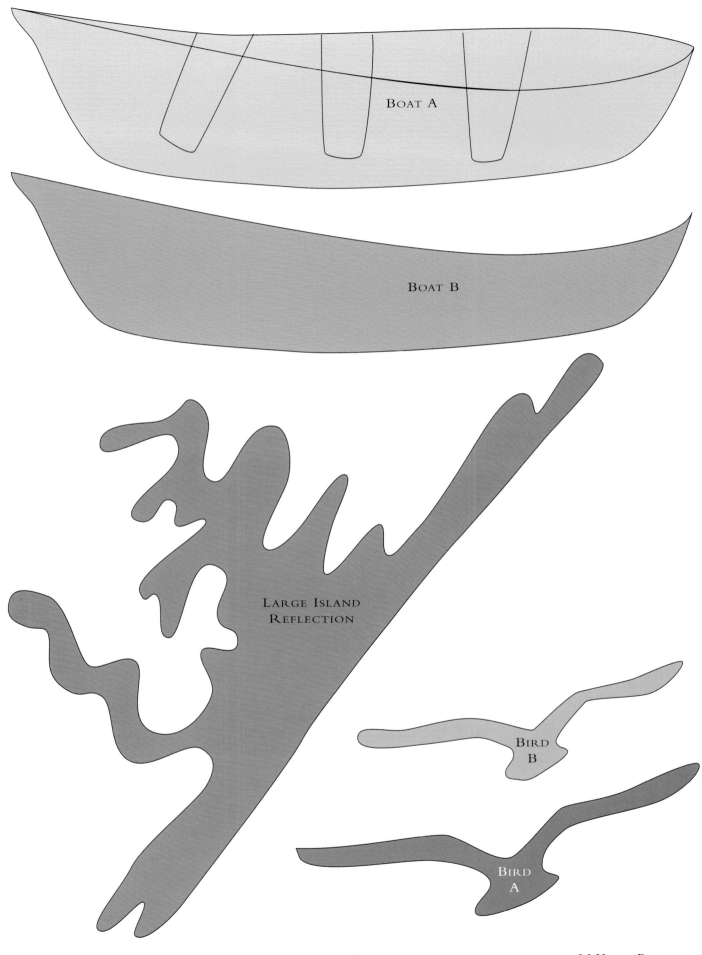

BOAT A

BOAT B

LARGE ISLAND
REFLECTION

BIRD
B

BIRD
A

LARGE ISLAND

TREE D

GRASS

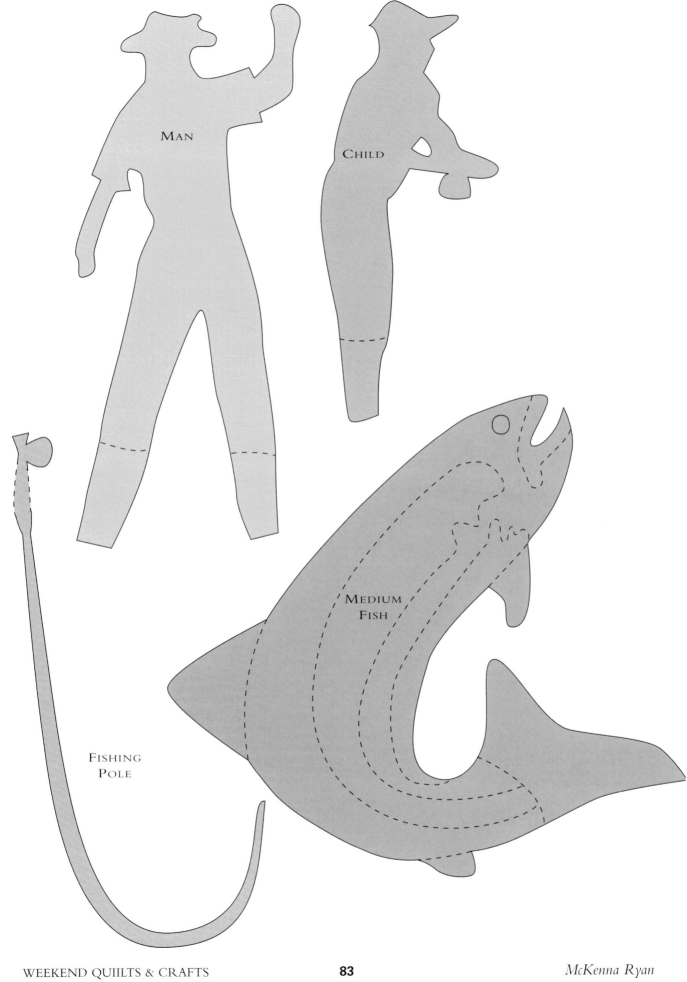

MAN

CHILD

MEDIUM
FISH

FISHING
POLE

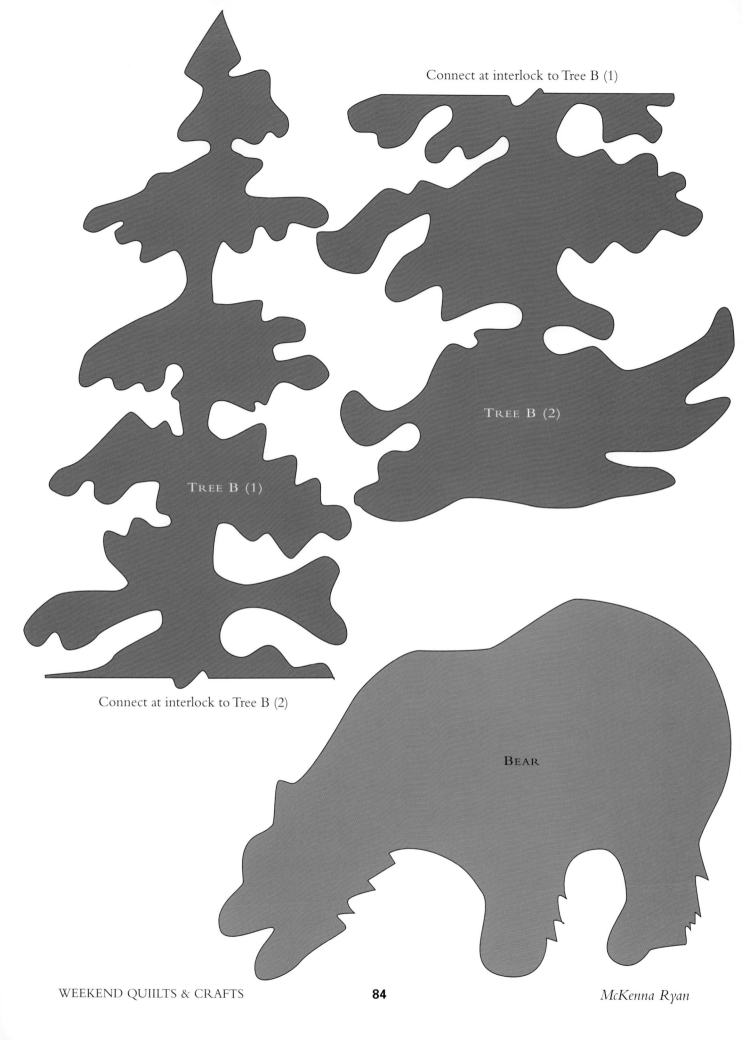

Connect at interlock to Tree B (1)

Tree B (2)

Tree B (1)

Connect at interlock to Tree B (2)

Bear

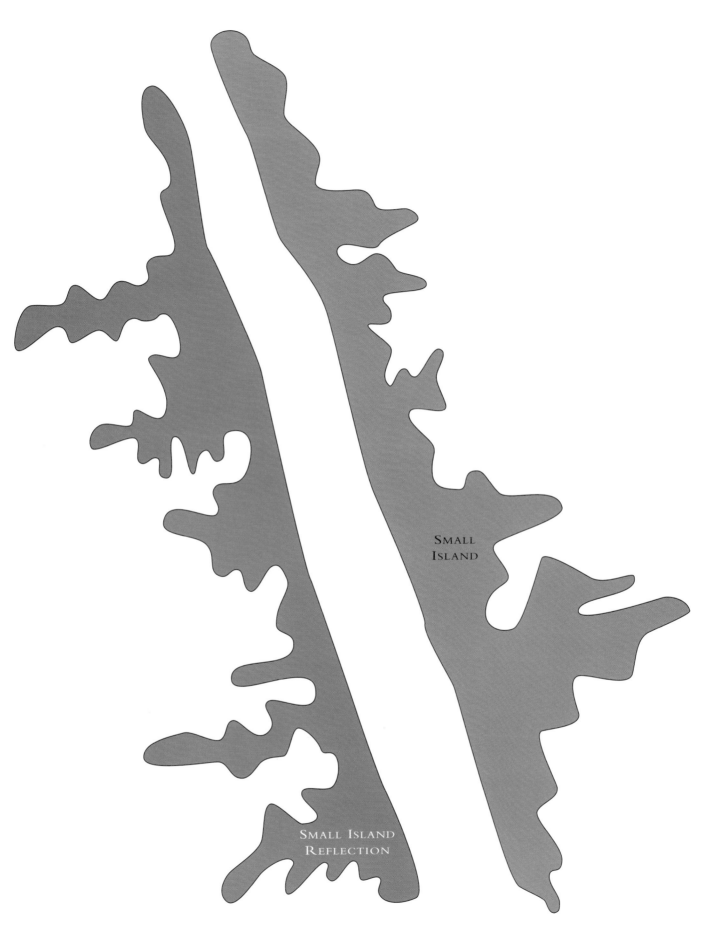

SMALL
ISLAND

SMALL ISLAND
REFLECTION

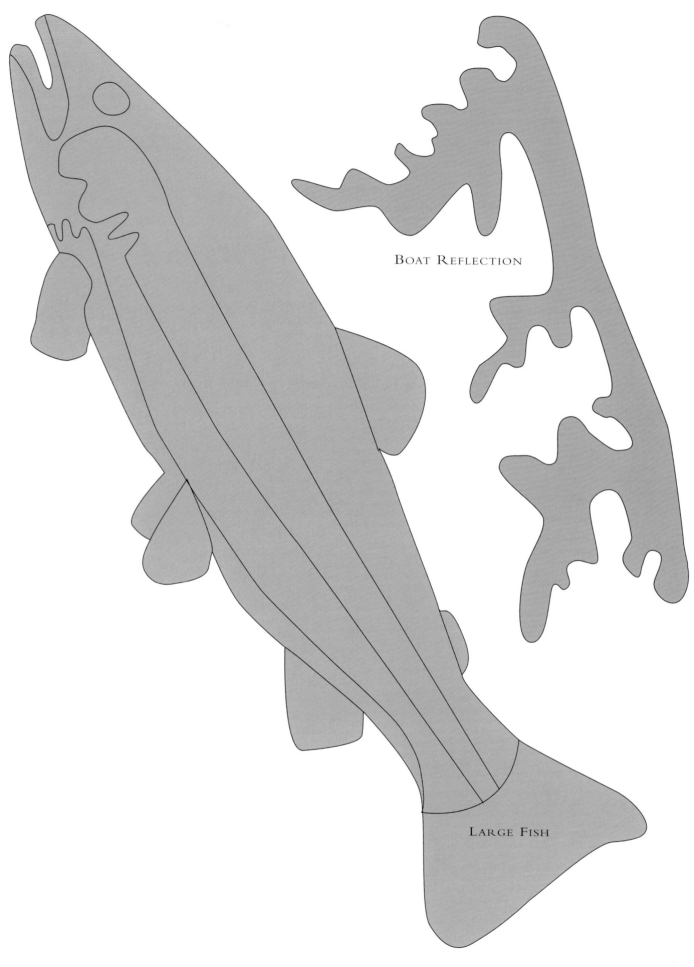

BOAT REFLECTION

LARGE FISH

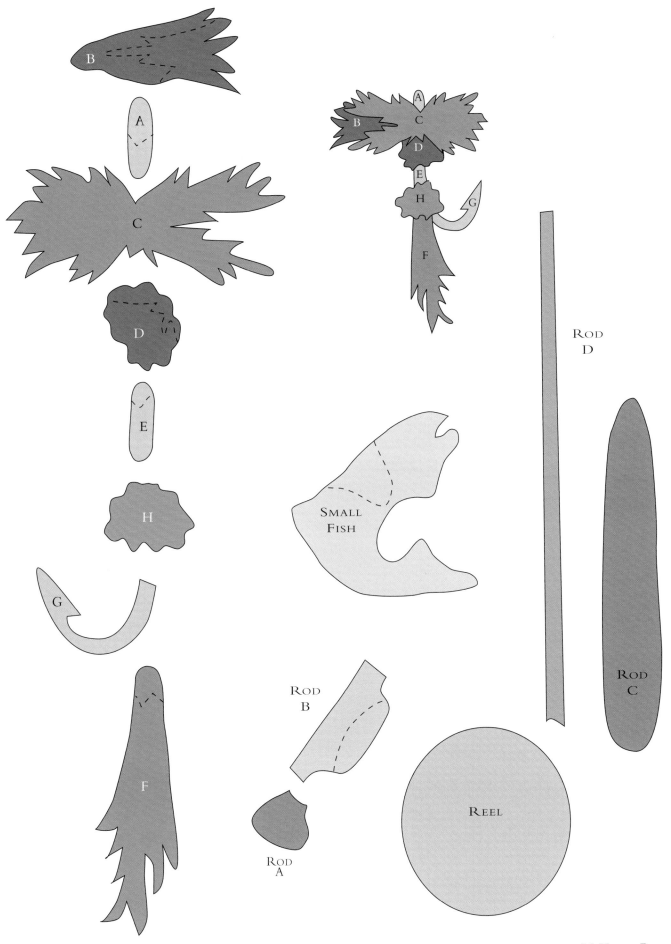

Deb Strain

MAKE A CHRISTMAS WISH

Happily settled in her Saltbox home studio in Ohio, artist Deb Strain delights in creating bright, cheery folk art tributes to country, gardens, home, and friendship. Her color palette, more intense than traditional folk art, depicts everyday scenes in a wonderfully warm-hearted way.

A former teacher, Deb once painted pattern packages for a friend. Encouraged by the positive response to her work, Deb produced cards that featured her own heartfelt designs, operating her budding business from home. Since then, Deb has experienced great success with prints and fabrics and is thrilled to see her artwork on an ever-increasing number of top-quality licensed products.

On the following pages you'll find projects ranging from the exuberant Celebrate wallhanging to a bed quilt, pillows, and door hanger all adapted from Deb's popular snow friends images.

Creating accents for your home gets you into the holiday spirit. Decorating with these artful designs adds style to your home. When the season is over, easily pack the fabric art pieces away to bring out and enjoy year after year—your own tradition in the making!

MATERIALS

- 1 yard red wool felt
- ½ yard green wool felt
- ½ yard gold wool felt
- 1¼ yards ¼-inch braid for border
- 1 yard lightweight fusible webbing
- ⅔ yard fabric for background sky
- ⅓ yard white print fabric for snow person
- ⅛ yard gray print fabric
- ¼ yard print fabric for scarf
- ¼ yard red fabric for vest and birds
- Small piece green Ultrasuede for vest trim
- Small piece of gold Ultrasuede for trim
- 7" square of Ultrasuede for stick arms
- Small piece orange fabric for nose
- Small piece of fabric for bird nest
- 6 medium size gold star buttons
- 2 large gold star buttons
- 2 gold stars for vest
- 16 small flat gold buttons
- 16 green beads
- 3 black buttons
- 30 clear seed beads
- Black, brown and red embroidery floss; #3 white pearl cotton
- Fabric marking pencil
- 18" x 21" piece of cotton batting
- Blush for cheeks
- Three ½" curtain rings
- 36" dowel rod (⁵⁄₁₆")

Celebrate Wallhanging

Finished size 21" x 24"

CUTTING & ASSEMBLY

1. Cut background fabric 18½" x 21½". Use the fabric marking pencil to trace "Celebrate" onto the background fabric.
2. Fuse webbing to the wrong side of gray print fabric. Cut the fabric 4" x 18½", slightly curving the edge. Fuse the piece to the background.
3. Using patterns provided, trace snow person, scarf, nose, birds, and bird nest to paper side of fusible webbing, following manufacturer's directions. Fuse the patterns to fabrics selected and cut out.

Deb Strain

4. Fuse snow person body to center of background. Fuse scarf in place. Fuse nose in place.

5. Using pattern provided and adding 1 inch on sides and bottom, cut out two vest pieces from red fabric. Use fusible webbing to make a 1-inch hem around the sides and bottom of each vest piece. Cut green Ultrasuede trim, using scalloped edge for vest pattern piece. Using a narrow zig-zag stitch, machine appliqué along front and bottom edges of vest. With black thread, machine feather stitch along two edges of each piece. Stitch green Ultrasuede in place, then machine appliqué around scallops with gold thread.

6. Cut out two flowerpot shapes from gold Ultrasuede. Tack in place on each side of the vest with one straight stitch. With black embroidery floss, make a tree shape design with running stitches above each flower pot. Tie floss in a

STEP 4

STEP 5

STEP 8

bow on the pot rim. Attach a gold star at top of each tree. Sew a gold button with a green bead to each scallop on the vest trim.

7. Machine appliqué along edges of snow person and nose. Lay vest in place and machine appliqué edge of scarf to hold vest in place. Complete scarf appliqué. Machine appliqué outer vest edges, leaving front and bottom of vest open.

8. Using pattern provided, cut out branches from brown Ultrasuede. Machine stitch in place. Fuse birds and bird nest in place. Machine appliqué birds and nest.

9. Using machine satin stitch and gold thread, stitch the word "Celebrate."

10. With brown embroidery floss, outline satin stitch letters with stem stitch. With black embroidery floss, make a big smile on the snow person with 8 French knots. Make a black French knot eye on each bird. Make black satin stitches on the cardinal. Straight stitch gold beaks on the birds.

11. Cut a small holly leaf from green felt. Attach it to the bird nest with a straight stitch. Make three red French knot berries.

12. Sew three buttons onto snow person. Make snowflakes on snow person body with white pearl cotton, making 4 straight stitches that overlap at the center. Sew a clear seed bead to the center of each snowflake.

13. Sew a large star button to each twig arm. Use brown embroidery floss to make "hangers" for the stars. Sew 6 gold star buttons randomly around the word "celebrate."

STEP 13

14. From green felt, cut two 3" x 22" strips and two 3" x 18" strips. Along the edges, cut 6 scallops on shorter pieces and 7 scallops on longer pieces.

15. Use the pattern to cut 24 stars from gold felt.

16. Using a zig-zag stitch and matching thread, sew a star to the center of each scallop. Stitch strips to the sides of the appliqué piece.

17. From red felt, cut a 24" x 28" rectangle. Place batting behind the appliqué center. Center the piece on the felt, batting between the two pieces. Machine quilt around the appliqué and stitch around the inside of the border.

18. Cut strips of braid; glue them along the seamline between background and green felt border.

19. Scallop the red felt to make a narrow border, using pinking shears. Sew curtain rings to the back of the wall hanging. Insert a dowel through the rings to hang.

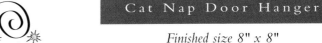

Cat Nap Door Hanger

Finished size 8" x 8"

MATERIALS

- ¼ yard lightweight fusible webbing
- ⅓ yard moons and stars fabric for background
- 8"-square of gold fabric for moon
- Small pieces of white, red, green, and gold fabrics for snowman, scarf, nightcap, and star
- Small pieces of beige and white Ultrasuede for cat
- 33 gold seed beads
- 5 larger gold beads
- 1 gold star bead
- 1 yard gold-and-white stripe cording
- 2½ yards ⅝" yellow satin ribbon
- 26" length of 1/4" elastic
- 8" cardboard circle
- 10" circle of muslin for backing
- Fabric glue
- 8" circle of white felt
- 8" circle of cotton batting
- Black and gold embroidery floss
- #3 white pearl cotton

CUTTING & ASSEMBLY

1. From background fabric cut a 10" circle.

2. Trace moon, star, snowman, scarf, cap, and cat patterns to fusible webbing. Fuse to appropriate fabrics for each piece. Cut out pieces. Remove paper backing as you fuse pieces to background fabric.

3. Fuse moon to background, then snowman body, scarf, hat, star, and cat.

4. Machine appliqué along fabric edges and to define design as shown on pattern pieces and photograph.

5. Machine stitch cat details as shown on pattern. Embroider additional details. With gold floss make nose using satin stitches outlined with stem stitch. Make snowman eyelids with two straight stitches and black floss. Embroider cat whiskers and mouth with straight stitches; make black French knots for eyes and nose. With white pearl cotton, make French knots on cat ears. Use straight stitches with pearl cotton to make a hanger to connect the star and the moon.

6. Sew gold seed beads on the moon. Sew larger gold beads to star points. Sew a gold star bead to the tip of the snowman's nightcap.

7. From muslin, cut a 10" circle. Layer muslin, cotton batting, and the appliqué piece; pin the layers together. Use contasting thread to machine quilt ¼" beyond the appliqué shape.

8. Center the appliqué piece on a cardboard circle, and pull fabric evenly to the back. Glue the fabric edges to the back of the cardboard.

9. Cut a 48" length of satin ribbon. Stitch a gathering line close to one edge. Gather threads to fit cardboard diameter. Stitch stripe cording to cover gathering line. Stitch cord and ribbon to the length of elastic.

10. Wrap and glue the ribbon edging around the fabric-covered cardboard edge. Overlap ends and secure to back of cardboard.

11. Fold remaining ribbon in half. Tack the fold to the back of the piece for hanging. Glue a white felt circle to the back to finish.

Finished size 16" x 6"

MATERIALS

For each pillow:

- ¾ yard fabric for back, border, and binding
- ½ yard muslin for backing
- ½ yard fusible webbing
- ½ yard fabric for sky background
- ½ yard fabric for moon
- Small pieces of white print for snow person
- Small piece of gold print fabric for star
- Black, green, and gold embroidery floss
- #3 white pearl cotton
- Blush for cheeks
- 2 yards cotton cording
- Two 16"-squares of cotton batting
- 16" square pillow form

Additional materials for Ski Buff Pillow

- Red fabric for sweater and hat
- 2 green print fabrics
- 1 small jingle bell

Additional materials for Snow Lady Pillow

- Red print fabric for jacket
- 2 green print fabrics for dress and scarf
- White fabric for birdhouse
- 2 gold star buttons
- Silk ribbon for ribbon roses or purchased flower appliqués

Additional materials for Marching Snowman Pillow

- 2 red print fabrics for vest and hat trim
- Green print for scarf
- Green Ultrasuede for vest trim
- 10 gold beads

CUTTING & ASSEMBLY

1. From red fabric, cut one 16½" square for pillow back, two 2" x 16½" border strips, and two 2" x 13½" border strips. Cut 1"-wide bias strips to total 66 inches when seamed together.
2. From muslin cut two 16½" squares for backing.
3. From background for sky, cut one 13½" square.

SKI BUFF PILLOW:

1. Using patterns provided, trace moon, star, legs, hands, face, hat, sweater, sweater band, sweater cuffs, scarf, and hat band to fusible webbing. Fuse webbing to fabrics for each piece and cut out each piece.
2. Remove paper backing as you fuse each piece. Fuse moon and star to background sky fabric. Fuse sweater, legs, and hands, scarf, face, and hat, then hat band, sweater band, and sweater cuffs.
3. Machine appliqué using coordinating threads over fabric edges and to define lines.

Deb Strain

4. Embroider details. Use gold satin stitches outlined with stem stitch for nose and sweater border. Make black French knot eyes. Add two straight stitches to attach star to moon. With white pearl cotton add French knots to hat band and sweater cuffs. Make snowflakes on sweater border with straight stitches.

5. Tack a jingle bell to the tip of the hat. Add a touch of blush to the cheeks.

6. Using 1/4" seams, stitch a 13½" border strip to each side. Stitch a 16½" border strip to top and bottom. Layer muslin, cotton batting, and pillow front. Machine quilt ¼" beyond the appliquéd design. Machine quilt in-the-ditch between the border and background fabric.

7. Insert cording in bias strips, or purchase cording, and sew to pillow front.

8. Place pillow backing and front right sides together. Stitch together, leaving an 8" opening to turn. Turn cover to right side, insert pillow form, and whipstitch opening closed.

SNOW LADY PILLOW:

1. Trace patterns for moon, star, legs, hands, face, jacket, dress, scarf, and birdhouse to fusible webbing. Fuse webbing to appropriate fabrics for each piece; cut out each piece.

2. Remove paper backing as you fuse each piece. Fuse moon and star, legs, dress, jacket, scarf, face and hands, and birdhouse in place.

3. Machine appliqué using coordinating threads over fabric edges; to make the pole, roof, and birdhouse base; and to define lines.

4. Embroider details. Use gold to satin stitch a nose and outline with stem stitch. Use black for eyes and heart-shape birdhouse door. Make two straight stitches to attach star to moon. Make eyes with French knots, and straight stitch brows. Satin stitch the heart on the birdhouse. Use green floss with stem and lazy daisy stitches for a vine on the birdhouse pole. Make a white pearl cotton French knot perch for the birdhouse.

5. Embroider silk ribbon flowers and leaves on birdhouse pole and on snow lady's head, or tack on purchased flower appliqués. Stitch two button stars on jacket. Add blush to her cheek!

6. Using ¼" seams, stitch a 13½" border strip to each side. Stitch a 16½" border strip to top and bottom. Layer muslin, batting, and pillow front. Machine quilt ¼" beyond the appliquéd design. Machine quilt in-the-ditch between the border and background fabric.

7. Insert cording in bias strips, or use purchased cording, and stitch to the pillow top edge, matching raw edges.

8. Place backing and front right sides together and stitch together, leaving an 8" opening to turn. Turn cover to right side, insert pillow form, and whipstitch opening closed.

MARCHING SNOWMAN PILLOW:

1. Trace moon, star, snowman body, vest, vest border, scarf, hat, and hat band to fusible webbing. Fuse webbing to fabrics for each piece; cut out each piece.

2. Remove paper backing as you fuse each piece. Fuse moon, snowman body, vest, scarf, vest border, hat, hat band, and star in place.

3. Machine appliqué using coordinating threads over fabric edges and to define lines.

4. Embroider details. Use gold to satin stitch nose, outline with stem stitch. Make mouth and eyes with black French knots. Add black straight

stitches for eye brows. Sew 10 gold beads to vest trim. Add a touch of blush to his cheek!

5. Using ¼" seams, stitch a 13½" border strip to each side. Stitch a 16½" border strip to top and bottom. Layer muslin, batting, and pillow front. Machine quilt ¼" beyond the appliquéd design. Machine quilt in-the-ditch between the border and background fabric.

6. Insert cording in bias strips, or purchase cording, and stitch to pillow front, matching raw edges.

7. Right sides together, stitch backing to pillow front, leaving an 8" opening to turn. Turn cover to right side, insert pillow form, and whipstitch opening closed.

Finished size 60" x 71½"

MATERIALS

- 4 yards backing fabric
- 1¾ yards dark blue stripe for blocks
- 1½ yards light blue print for blocks
- 1½ yards blue with gold tar print
- 2 yards gold print for star points, centers, and binding
- 66" x 78" cotton batting
- Pearl cotton to tie quilt

CUTTING & ASSEMBLY

1. From dark blue stripe, cut 150—3½" squares. From light blue print, cut 120—3½" squares.

2. From gold, cut 42—3" squares. Using Pattern A, cut 142 points; reverse the pattern and cut 142 points.

3. Also from gold fabric, cut 7—2½"-wide strips. Sew the strips together end to end to make a continuous length to use for the binding.

4. From blue with gold star print, cut 71 of Pattern B.

5. Sew together 3 rows of 3½" dark blue and light blue squares, referring to the illustration for placement. Press seams toward dark blue squares. Sew together the rows to make a 9½" square, including seam allowance. Make 30 Nine-Patch blocks.

6. Sew four Pattern A points to each Pattern B piece, noting placement. Press seams toward the gold fabric. Repeat to make 71 units.

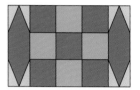

7. Lay out 6 rows of Nine-Patch blocks with point units alongside the blocks. Sew the rows together.

8. Lay out 7 rows using the remaining point units and the 3" gold squares, placing squares between each unit and at the end of the units.

9. Lay out the rows of point units with gold squares and the rows of Nine-Patch blocks with point units, beginning and ending with a row of point units with gold squares. Sew the rows together, butting seams for a neat finish. Press the seams in one direction.

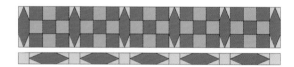

10. Cut and piece backing fabric to measure at least 3" larger all around than the quilt top. Press the seams in one direction.

12. Lay out the backing on a smooth surface, wrong side up, and secure it in place. Fluff and layer the batting. Place the quilt top right side up on the layers; pin or baste through all layers.

13. Use pearl cotton to tie at the corners of the gold star squares.

14. Fold the binding in half lengthwise and press. Raw edges together, sew the binding to the quilt top using a ¼" seam, mitering the corners and overlaping the binding ends. Turn the binding to the backing and hand stitch the folded edge to the backing.

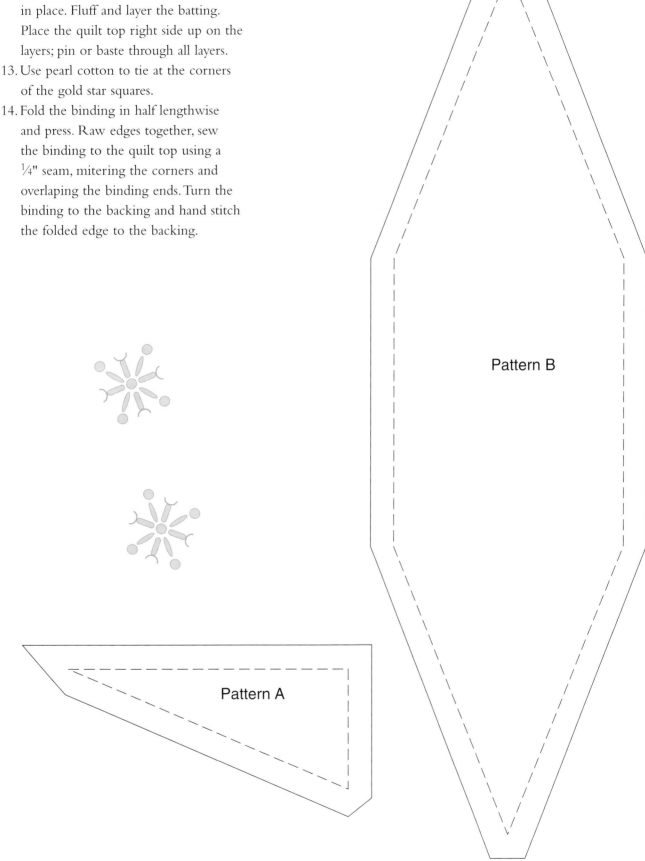

Pattern B

Pattern A

Enlarge patterns by 200%

Ski Buff Pillow

Snow Lady Pillow

Ski Buff Pillow

Marching Snowman Pillow

Enlarge patterns by 200%

Marching Snowman Pillow

Margaret Sindelar

A NEW HAND IN OURS

Margaret Ann Sindelar's remarkable 30-year career as a needlework teacher, designer, and photo-stylist for book and magazine publishers is due in large part to her enduring admiration for the legendary Annie Oakley. After an aunt expanded Margaret's middle name to Annie, the Oakley soon followed to become a nickname that stuck.

And just what do a Wild-West "gunslinger" and a 20th century woman with a Master's Degree in Family Economics and Management have in common? Margaret's research reveals interesting parallels in their lives. While Oakley's sewing skills were learned in an orphanage and Margaret's were developed through a college curriculum, both developed a lifelong love of the needlearts.

For shooting competitions Annie always wore a lucky-star badge. While on the road with her Wild West show, Oakley designed and made the elaborate beaded and fringed show costumes and filled her trunk with embroidery and fancy needlework.

Margaret Sindelar has followed Annie Oakley's footsteps to create similar works of enduring art, through her design company—Cottonwood Classics—and by wearing her own lucky star badge!

MATERIALS

- 2 yards of bright blue fabric for ruffle and back
- 1 yard of baby print fabric for outer border
- $\frac{1}{2}$ yard of cream fabric for center panel
- $\frac{1}{2}$ yard of hot pink fabric for inner border
- $\frac{1}{2}$ yard of lime green fabric for piping
- Scraps of assorted pink fabrics for yo-yo flowers
- $25\frac{1}{2}$" x 27" batting
- $3\frac{1}{2}$ yards of $\frac{1}{8}$" cording
- $6\frac{1}{4}$ yards of flat rosebud trim
- $1\frac{3}{4}$ yards of 4mm blue silk ribbon
- $2\frac{1}{4}$ yards of 7mm green silk ribbon
- Light, medium, and dark pink pearl cotton
- Pink rayon thread
- Fusible web

Monday's Child Quilt

Finished size $31\frac{1}{2}$" x 33" including Ruffle

CUTTING

1. From the bright blue fabric, cut a $26\frac{1}{4}$" x $27\frac{3}{4}$" rectangle for the quilt back. Cut five $6\frac{3}{4}$" x 44" strips for the ruffle.

2. From the baby print fabric, cut two $5\frac{5}{8}$" x $30\frac{1}{2}$" strips and two $5\frac{5}{8}$" x 32" strips for the borders.

3. From the cream fabric, cut a 15" x 17" rectangle for the center panel. You will trim this to size after the embroidery is complete.

4. From the hot pink fabric, cut a $16\frac{1}{2}$" x 18" rectangle for the center panel.

5. From the lime green fabric, cut enough $1\frac{1}{4}$"-wide bias strips to cover the cording. Sew the strips together into one long strip.

Monday's child is fair of face,
Tuesday's child is full of grace,
Wednesday's child is full of woe,
Thursday's child has far to go.
Friday's child is loving and giving,
Saturday's child works hard for his living,
And the child born on the Sabbath day,
Is bonny and blithe, and good and gay.

EMBROIDER THE CENTER PANEL

1. Machine embroider the poem (page 113) in the center of the cream rectangle, or take the fabric to a local custom embroidery shop (the kind of shop that makes custom T-shirts and caps) and have it stitched for you. Use a contrasting color thread to highlight the baby's day of birth.

2. Fuse the embroidered rectangle to a piece of fusible web. Making sure the embroidery is centered, trim the rectangle to 13½" x 15". Use the corner template on page 117 to trim the corners, if desired.

3. Center the embroidered rectangle on the pink rectangle, and fuse. Using the pink rayon thread, machine satin stitch around the edge of the center panel.

4. Referring to the photo, use the blue silk ribbon to sew a long running stitch just inside the edge of the center panel.

5. Use the pink fabric scraps to make 13 yo-yo flowers. To make a yo-yo flower, cut a 3¼"-diameter circle from fabric. Turn under ¼" to the wrong side, and hand-sew a line of gathering stitches around the edge. Pull the thread to gather the circle. Holding the gathered side up, use pearl cotton to make to several French knots in the center of the flower.

6. Cut 6" lengths of the green ribbon and loop each into a figure 8. Center a yo-yo flower on each ribbon loop and hand-stitch them together. Referring to the photo, arrange the 13 flowers on the center panel and hand-stitch in place.

ASSEMBLE THE QUILT

1. With right sides together and using a ¼" seam allowance, sew the borders to the center panel, starting and stopping the seams ¼" away from the edge of the panel.

2. Working on one corner at a time, place one border on top of the adjacent border as shown in Diagram A. Fold the top border under so that it forms a 45-degree angle; press the fold.

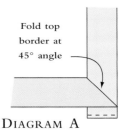

Fold top border at 45° angle

DIAGRAM A

3. Fold the quilt top right sides together, matching the border edges. Sew along the fold line from the corner out to the edge of the border. See Diagram B.

4. Unfold the quilt top and check to make sure the miter is flat. Trim the seam allowance to ¼". Repeat for all four corners. Press the borders, then round the corners slightly.

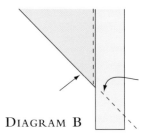

DIAGRAM B

5. Using a zipper foot and a ½" seam allowance, cover the cording with the green fabric strip. Trim the seam allowance to 3⁄8". Baste the piping to the quilt top.

6. Sew the ruffle strips together into one long strip; stitch the ends together to make a loop. Fold in half lengthwise, wrong sides together; press. Stitch the rosebud trim about ¼" in from the folded edge.

7. Sew two rows of gathering stitches along the raw edge of the ruffle strip. Gather the ruffle to fit the quilt top; pin and baste in place on top of the piping.

8. Pin the batting to the wrong side of the quilt top. With the batting against the machine, stitch the batting and quilt top together, stitching the piping and ruffle in place at the same time. Remove the basting stitches.

9. Place the backing face down on the quilt top, with the ruffle between the layers and out of the seam area; pin. With the batting against the machine, sew the layers together with a ⅜" seam allowance, leaving a 10" opening along one side for turning. Turn right side out through the opening; hand-stitch the opening closed.

10. Hand-tack at corners through backing to hold all layers together.

Monday's child is fair of face

Tuesday's child is full of grace

Wednesday's child is full of woe

Thursday's child has far to go

Friday's child is loving and giving

Saturday's child works hard for a living

And the child born on the Sabbath day

Is bonny and blithe, and good and gay.

*Finished size 17" square
including Ruffle*

MATERIALS

- 1 yard of bright blue fabric for patchwork, ruffle, and back

- $\frac{1}{4}$ yard of dark blue fabric for patchwork

- $\frac{1}{4}$ yard of hot pink fabric for patchwork and piping

- Assorted pink fabric scraps for yo-yo flowers

- $1\frac{1}{2}$ yards of $\frac{3}{8}$"-wide pink double-faced satin ribbon

- 1 yard of 7mm green silk ribbon

- Light, medium, and dark pink pearl cotton

- $1\frac{1}{2}$ yards of $\frac{1}{8}$" cording

- 12" square pillow form

CUTTING

1. From the bright blue fabric, cut three $5\frac{3}{4}$" x 42" strips for the ruffle and one $12\frac{3}{4}$" square for the back. Using the patterns on page 117, cut nine A diamonds. Be sure to transfer the dots from the pattern to the wrong side of each fabric piece.

2. From the dark blue fabric, cut nine A diamonds, two C pieces, and two D pieces using the patterns on page 117.

3. From the hot pink fabric, cut eight A diamonds, two B pieces, two C pieces, and two D pieces. Cut enough

$1\frac{1}{4}$"-wide bias strips to cover the piping cord. Sew the bias strips together into one long strip.

PIECE THE PILLOW TOP

1. Referring to Diagram C, sew the dark blue and bright blue diamonds together in strips. Start and stop the seams at the dots, backstitching at both ends. Press the seams open.

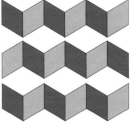

DIAGRAM C

2. Set-in the pink diamonds to complete the Tumbling Block. To set-in the pieces, place a pink diamond right sides together with a dark blue or bright

blue diamond, matching the dots. Pin the pieces, and sew from dot to dot, starting at the outside edge and sewing in toward the seam between the blue diamonds. Stop with the needle down between the two blue diamonds; the needle should be in the pink fabric only. See Diagram D.

DIAGRAM D

3. With the needle down, pivot the pieces, match the adjacent side of the pink diamond to the second blue diamond, and finish sewing the seam, stopping at the dot. See Diagram E.

DIAGRAM E

4. Referring to Diagram F for correct placement, set-in the B, C, and D pieces to complete the pillow top.

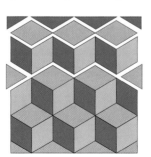

DIAGRAM F

5. Using dark pink pearl cotton floss, make a French knot at each intersection of diamonds.

6. Referring to Steps 5 and 6 in Embroider the Center Panel on page 113, make six yo-yo flowers from assorted pink fabric scraps, referring to the photos at left. Arrange the yo-yos and ribbon loops on the pillow top as desired, and hand-stitch in place.

ASSEMBLE THE PILLOW

1. Using a zipper foot and a ½" seam allowance, cover the cord with the pink strip. Trim the seam allowance to ⅜". Baste the piping in place around the edge of the pillow top.

2. Sew the ruffle strips together into one long strip; sew the ends together to make a loop. Fold the strip in half lengthwise, wrong sides together; press. Sew two rows of gathering stitches along the raw edge of the ruffle fabric.

3. Divide the ruffle into quarters and mark. Pin the quarter points to the corners of the pillow top, and gather the ruffle to fit. Pin, then baste the ruffle in place on top of the piping.

4. Place the pillow back face down on the pieced top, with the ruffle between the layers and out of the seam area. Stitch with a ⅜" seam allowance, leaving an opening along one side for turning and stuffing.

5. Turn right side out through the opening. Insert the pillow form, and stitch the opening closed.

6. Cut the pink satin ribbon into two equal lengths. Tie a small knot in each end of both ribbons. Place one ribbon on top of the other, and hand-tack the center of the ribbons to the center of the pillow. Tie a teething ring in the ribbons as shown in the photo.

Baby Blocks

Finished size 14" square

MATERIALS

For three blocks:

- 1/8 yard each or large scraps of the following fabrics: blue-and-yellow plaid, green-and-pink plaid, blue check, blue print, green print, and pink print

- 8" square of muslin

- Blue, yellow, light pink, dark pink, light green, and dark green pearl cotton

- Three 4¼" x 4¼" x 4¼" foam cubes

- Photo transfer paper for color laser copiers

CUTTING

1. From the blue-and-yellow plaid, green-and-pink plaid, and blue check fabrics, cut five 3½" squares each.

2. From the blue, green, and pink print fabrics, cut twelve 3" squares each. Cut each square in half diagonally.

ASSEMBLY

1. Following the manufacturer's instructions, transfer three 3" square photo images onto the muslin square. Be sure to leave at least ½" between the images. Cut the muslin into 3½" squares.

2. Sew a print triangle to opposite sides of each photo transfer square; press. Sew triangles to the two remaining sides of each square, and press. See Diagram G.

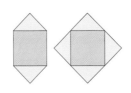

DIAGRAM G

3. In the same manner, sew coordinating print triangles to each plaid square; press.

4. Sew three pieced squares and a photo square together in a strip, as shown in Diagram H. Bring the edges of the first and last squares right sides together and sew, forming a loop.

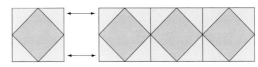

DIAGRAM H

5. With right sides together, pin a matching square to one end of the loop. Stitch the square to the loop, creating the bottom of the block. For best results, stop stitching each seam ¼" from the corner, lower the needle into the fabric, pivot the fabric, and stitch the next side.

6. In the same manner, pin the remaining square to the opposite end of the block. Stitch two adjacent sides only at this time.

7. Turn the block right side out. Insert a foam cube into the block, and whipstitch the last two sides closed.

8. Thread a needle with two different colors of pearl cotton. Take a single stitch at the midpoint of each edge, at the corners of the plaid squares. Tie a double knot and clip the threads, leaving ½" tails.

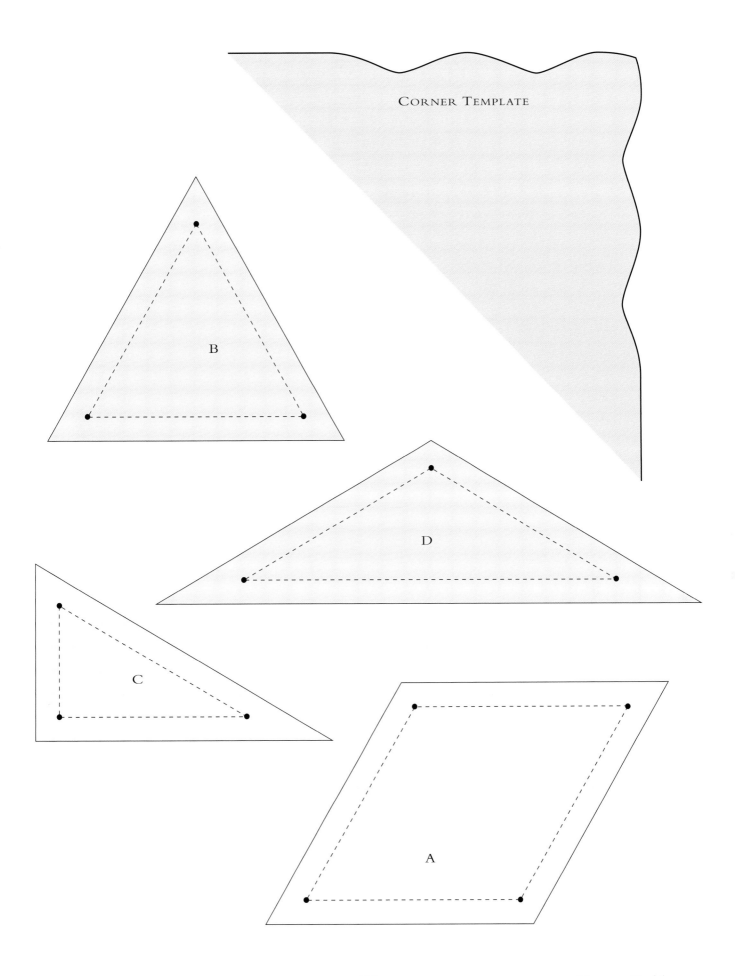

CORNER TEMPLATE

B

D

C

A

Margaret Sindelar

CHRISTMAS WITH A TWIST

When crafts-designer Margaret Sindelar set out to decorate her guest room for the holidays, her goal was to "create a warm and cozy room where someone would feel especially welcome." But Margaret had other, more practical goals, as well. She decided that whatever she designed had to meet certain requirements: It had to be fast and easy, incorporate traditional patterns, and use classic Christmas colors. On top of all that, it had to be reversible so that she could use it throughout the year.

With her checklist in hand, Margaret created this wonderful bedroom ensemble. The simple shapes make construction quick and easy, and the classic colors mean it will never go out of style. The fact that the pieces are reversible means you get two complete looks for the work of one.

Margaret's children are pretty spread-out these days, with a daughter in Denver, a son at the University of Iowa, and another daughter and son-in-law serving in the Peace Corps in Slovakia. She looks forward to the holidays, when they'll all come home to visit. "The only problem is," Margaret says, "everyone's lives are so busy, I'm not sure we'll all be here at the same time. In any event, I have a feeling this room will get lots of use!"

MATERIALS

- 3 yards of cream fabric for blocks
- 2⅝ yards of red fabric for blocks and sashing
- 2⅜ yards of green fabric for blocks and binding
- 2 yards of green print fabric for corner squares and outer border
- ⅝ yard of dark green fabric for inner border
- 6 yards of contrasting fabric for back
- Queen-size batting
- Thirty 1" red buttons
- Thirty 1" buttons to coordinate with backing fabric
- Pearl cotton

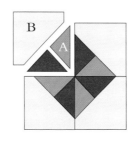

DIAGRAM A

Quick-Sew Quilt

Finished size 82" x 95"

CUTTING

1. From the cream fabric, cut one hundred twenty 5½" squares.

2. From the red fabric, cut sixty 3¾" squares; cut diagonally for two A triangles. Cut seventy-one 3½" x 10½" sashing strips.

3. From the green fabric, cut sixty 3¾" squares; cut diagonally for two A triangles. Cut nine 6" x 44" binding strips.

4. From the green print, cut nine 5½" x 44" strips. Cut forty-two 3½" corner squares.

5. From the dark green fabric, cut eight 1½" x 44" strips.

ASSEMBLY

1. Make a template for B from the pattern on page 126. Place the template on a cream square, align the edges, and trim off the corner. Repeat for all cream squares.

2. Sew a red and a green A triangle together as shown in Diagram A. Sew this unit to a B piece to form a square. Repeat with all remaining red and green triangles and B pieces, making sure the colors are correctly placed each time.

3. Referring to Diagram A, sew four of

119

Margaret Sindelar

the squares together to form a Star Wheel block. Make 30 blocks.

4. Assemble the blocks and sashing strips into rows as shown in Diagram B. Sew the remaining sashing strips and corner squares into alternate rows. Sew the rows together.

5. Sew the 1½"-wide dark green strips end-to-end in pairs. Add the strips to the quilt top, mitering the corners. In the same manner, sew the 5½"-wide green strips together, piecing as needed to achieve the required length. Add them to the quilt top, mitering the corners.

6. Piece the backing fabric. Layer the backing, batting, and quilt top, and baste. Using the pearl cotton, sew a red button to the center of each block, and sew a corresponding button at the same spot on the back of the quilt. Machine-quilt along the edge of the inner border.

7. Trim the backing and batting so that they are ¾" larger than the quilt top on all sides. Prepare the binding strips, referring to the General Instructions for mitered binding on page 7. Pin the binding to the quilt, having the edges even with the batting and backing. Stitch the binding in place with a 1" seam allowance. Bring the folded edges to the back of the quilt and whipstitch in place.

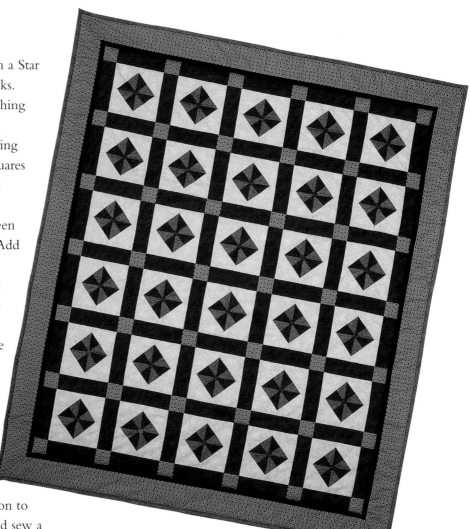

DIAGRAM B

ROOM-SIZE ROLE REVERSAL

Get two decorating looks at once by making your bedroom ensemble reversible. The items shown in this photo are simply the reverse of those featured on page 119. The back of the Star Wheel quilt is a pretty floral fabric that coordinates with the binding and with the green plaid on the Santa pillow. The bolster pillow is a sumptuous accent that's a snap to make. Simply measure the circumference of the pillow and add several inches for overlap and seam allowances. Measure the width and add about 12". Cut two rectangles of fabric—one to coordinate with each side of the quilt. Place the rectangles right sides together and stitch with a ¼" seam allowance, leaving an opening for turning. Turn right side out, stitch the opening closed, and press. On one short end, add a row of buttonholes, and on the other end, sew a corresponding row of back-to-back buttons. Wrap the rectangle around the pillow, button it on, and tie each end with a tasseled chair tie. The envelope pillow is even easier: Make a two-sided pillowcase that's the width of the pillow and 1½ times its length. Insert the pillow in the case, and fold the excess over as a flap. Add a row of buttons to the flap for a decorative touch.

WEEKEND QUIILTS & CRAFTS   **121**   *Margaret Sindelar*

20" square

MATERIALS

- 1¼ yards of green plaid fabric for ruffle and back
- Fat quarter or large scrap of tan fabric for background
- ⅛ yard each of red and red-and-green print fabrics for patchwork
- Large scraps of red, white-on-white, and flesh color fabrics for appliqués
- Scraps of red, pink, peach, green, and white fabrics for appliqués
- Fusible web
- Fabric stabilizer
- 2 yards of red sew-in piping
- Black and blue embroidery floss
- Red, white, gray, peach, and pink rayon thread
- 14" square pillow form
- Five red beads
- 24 small black bugle beads
- Large red jingle bell
- Powder blush

CUTTING

1. From the green plaid fabric, cut a 14½" square. Cut 7"-wide bias strips, and sew them together end-to-end to make a 120" strip.
2. From the tan fabric, cut a 9½" square.
3. From the red fabric, cut four 3" squares. From the red-and-green print fabric, cut four 3" x 9½" rectangles.
4. Refer to the General Instructions on page 6 to trace, apply fusible web to, and cut out the following appliqué pieces from the scrap fabrics: Santa's hat, hat trim, holly leaves, face, eyebrows, cheeks, mustache, mouth, and beard. Cut out the white part of each eye only; the irises are stitched with floss.

ASSEMBLY

1. Sew a 3" x 9½" rectangle to opposite sides of the tan square. Sew a red square to each end of the two remaining rectangles; sew these to the top and bottom of the pillow top.
2. Center the appliqué pieces on the pillow top. For best results, remove the backing and position all the pieces, checking their placement, before fusing any of them. Fuse. Line the pillow top with stabilizer. Machine-appliqué around all pieces using satin

stitches and matching rayon threads. Satin-stitch the eyes with blue floss. With black floss, add French knot pupils and straight-stitch eyelashes. Sew on red beads for holly berries and black bugle beads to decorate the hat trim.

3. Pin the piping to the right side of the pillow top, aligning the raw edges. Stitch with a ¼" seam allowance.

4. To make the ruffle, fold the 120" strip in half lengthwise, wrong sides together, and press. Sew a long gathering stitch ¼" from the raw edge. Divide the ruffle into quarters and mark. Place the ruffle on the pillow top, right sides together, raw edges even, and quarter marks pinned at the midpoint of each side. Pull the gathering thread so the ruffle fits the pillow top. Stitch the ruffle in place on top of the piping.

5. Place the pillow front and back right sides together with the ruffle inside, out of the seam area. Stitch with a ¼" seam allowance, leaving an opening for turning. Trim the corners, and turn right side out. Insert the pillow form. Stitch the opening closed. Stitch the jingle bell to the hat and add powder blush to cheeks and nose.

Star Wheel Tree Garland

Approximately 48"

MATERIALS

- Scraps of red, green, tan, and red-and-green print fabrics
- 14" x 16" sheet each of red and green card stock paper
- Fusible web
- The following beads: sixteen 18 x 21mm moss oval; sixteen 14 x 8.5mm moss cushion; thirteen 18 x 21mm red clay oval; eight 18 x 11mm gold cushion; seven 6mm gold round; seven 25mm sunburst
- Fifteen ½" gold sleigh bells
- 2 yards of red cotton craft string
- Red and gold embroidery floss
- Pinking shears
- Tapestry needle

ASSEMBLY

1. Referring to the General Instructions on page 6, apply fusible web to and cut out sixteen 1½" red fabric squares and sixteen 1½" green fabric squares. Cut each square in half diagonally. Trim the edges with pinking shears.

2. Arrange the triangles into the Star Wheel design on a piece of green paper as shown in Diagram C, leaving a slight space between the pieces. Fuse the triangles to the paper. Cut out the green paper square with pinking shears, cutting ⅛" outside the design.

3. Fuse the green square to a piece of red paper. Using pinking shears, cut out the red paper, cutting ⅛" outside the green paper. Repeat to make three more Star Wheel blocks.

4. To make the trees, trace the outline of the tree pattern from page 129 onto red paper. Trace, apply fusible web to, and cut out nine green triangles,

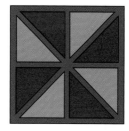

DIAGRAM C

18 red-and-green print triangles, and three tan trunks. Trim the pieces with pinking shears. Arrange them on the red paper, leaving a slight space between the pieces; fuse. With pinking shears, cut out along the traced lines.

5. Fuse the red tree onto green paper. Using pinking shears, cut out ⅛" from the design. Make two more trees.

6. Make a knot approximately 12" from one end of the craft string. Using the photo as a guide, string the beads in the following order: red clay oval, moss oval, moss cushion, gold cushion, moss cushion, moss oval, red clay oval. Leave a space for a Star Wheel block, then repeat the sequence twice, then leave another space. Continue in this manner until all the beads have been strung. Knot the string, leaving approximately 12" free at the end.

7. Thread the tapestry needle with gold floss. Sew a sunburst bead onto the center of a Star Wheel block, securing it with a gold bead. Tie the block onto the garland with red floss.

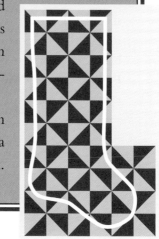

STAR WHEEL STOCKING

Use the Star Wheel block to make a patchwork front for your favorite stocking pattern. Simply make enough complete blocks to cover the stocking pattern, plus seam allowances. Sew the blocks together as shown in the diagram. Pin the stocking pattern to the patchwork and cut out around the pattern. (The stocking shown was made extra long so that the top could be turned down as a cuff.) Cut a back and two lining pieces from contrasting fabric, and assemble the stocking.

Embellish the stocking as desired. The one shown has red sew-in piping around the edges, and a pretty gold bead at the center of each block.

Margaret Sindelar

8. Using gold floss, stitch five gold sleigh bells to each tree. Add a sunburst and bead at the top. Tie the tree to a red clay bead on the garland. Add two trees and three Star Wheel blocks to complete the garland.

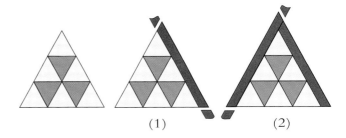

(1)   (2)

DIAGRAM D

Triangle Tree Table Topper

24" diameter

MATERIALS

- 1¼ yards of red fabric for sashing, back, and binding
- ⅜ yard of red-and-green print fabric for patchwork
- ¼ yard of green fabric for patchwork
- ⅛ yard or large scrap of tan fabric for patchwork
- 26" square of thin batting
- Six 1" gold star buttons
- Ten each red, green, and gold ¼" sleigh bells
- Twenty-four 2½" gold tassels

CUTTING

1. From red fabric, cut a 26" square and four 1½" x 44" strips. Cut six E and six E reverse pieces using the pattern on page 127. Cut enough 1½"-wide bias strips to make 80" of binding.
2. From the red-and-green print fabric, cut 36 C triangles.
3. From the green fabric, cut 18 C triangles.
4. From the tan fabric, cut six D pieces.

ASSEMBLY

1. Referring to the photo, sew the triangles together in rows, then sew the rows together to form the larger triangle.
2. Place a 1½" x 44" red strip face down on the right-hand side of the pieced triangle, aligning the raw edges. Stitch with a ¼" seam allowance, and press the strip open. Trim the top and bottom even with the triangle, as shown in Diagram D(1). In the same manner, place the strip on the left side of the triangle. Stitch, press, and trim the excess as shown in Diagram D(2).

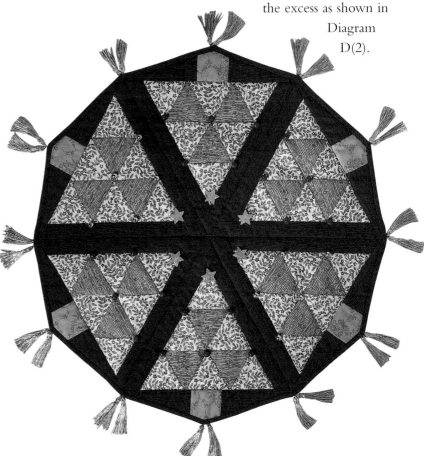

3. Sew the E and E reverse pieces to opposite sides of the tan D trunk. Stitch the trunk section to the tree as shown in Diagram E. Repeat to make five more triangle trees.

4. Sew the triangle trees together in two sets of three, then join the halves to complete the quilt top. Layer the backing, batting, and quilt top, and baste. Machine quilt as desired. Finish the outside edge with a ¼" bias binding, preparing the strips as directed on page 7 in the General Instructions.

5. Sew five sleigh bells to each tree and add a star button at the top. Add two tassels to the outside edge at each tree trunk and sashing seam.

DIAGRAM E

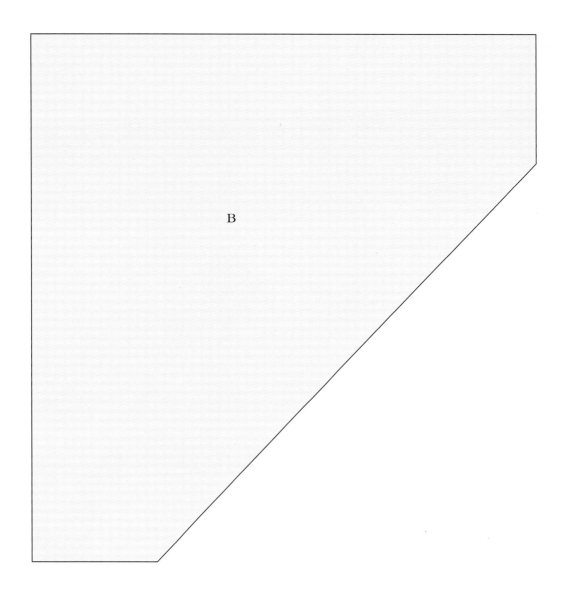

B

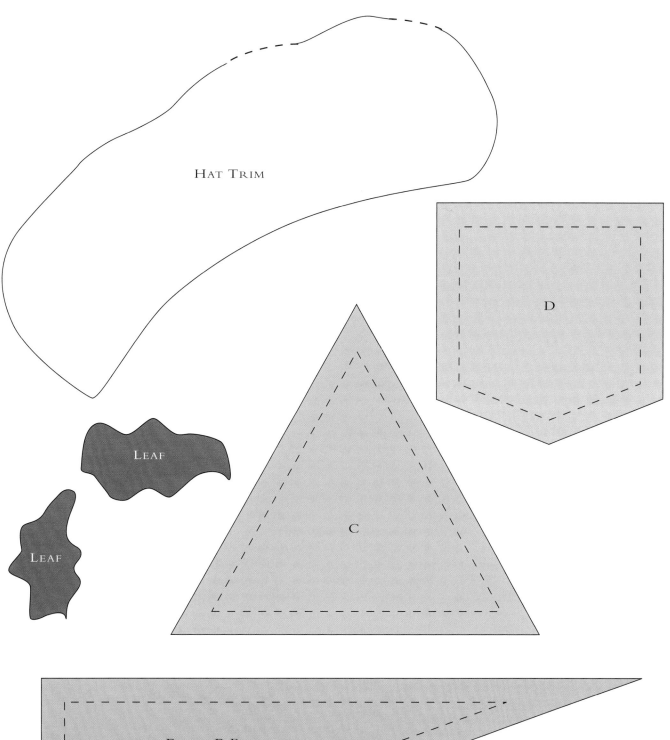

HAT TRIM

D

LEAF

LEAF

C

E AND E REVERSE

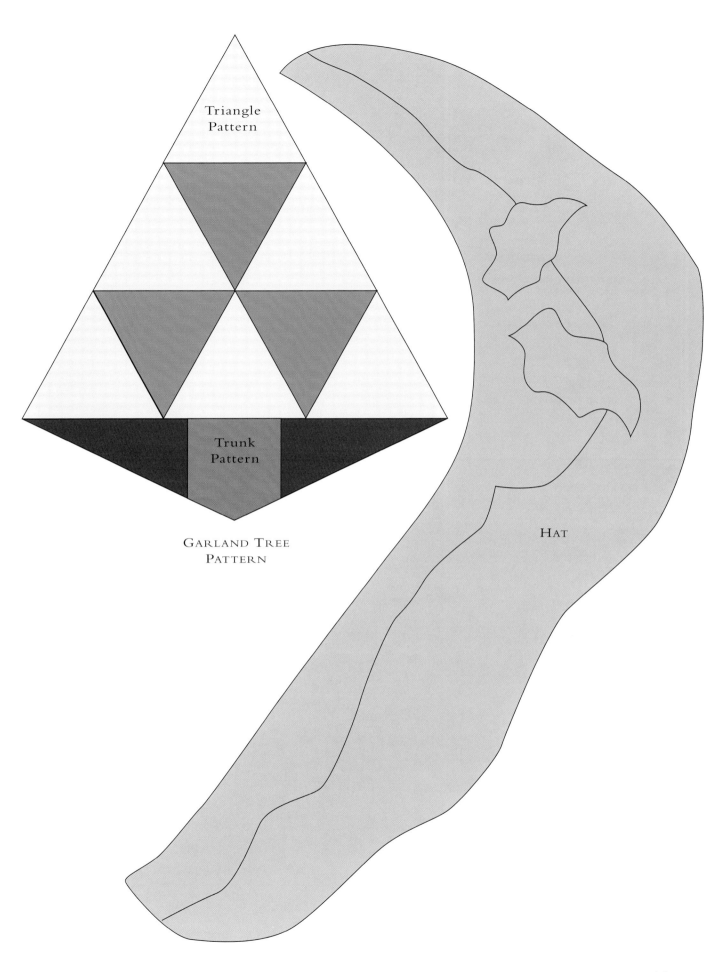

Triangle
Pattern

Trunk
Pattern

GARLAND TREE
PATTERN

Hat

Suellen Wassem

WILDFLOWER WEDDING

It was a happy coincidence that Suellen's son and future daughter-in-law, Heath and Becky, were planning their wedding just as she was designing this collection. Their plans provided not only inspiration but the color scheme and theme, as well. The colors co-ordinate with the bridesmaids' navy blue dresses. And the wildflowers are Suellen's way of fulfilling the bride's wish: It seems Becky wants wildflowers at her wedding, but cannot have them because of her sister's allergies. Suellen's solution was to work the wildflowers into the collection. The wildflower motif may also help to remind the wedding guests of the season. An early spring wedding is planned but, Suellen says, "Since the wedding is in Rochester, New York, I'm afraid it might be spring only in our imaginations!"

Suellen's charming collection of keepsakes makes a perfect wedding gift. Guests can record their names and sentiments in the guest book or on the wallhanging itself. An album provides ample room for photos and mementos, and the keepsake box is a special place to store small treasures.

MATERIALS

- 3½ yards of navy print fabric for borders, backing, and binding
- ⅞ yard of cream solid for piecing
- ¼ yard each of the following fabrics for piecing and appliqués: two different red prints, red mini check, red homespun, tan homespun, blue plaid, blue print, green homespun, and black print
- Scraps of 20 to 30 medium and dark print and plaid fabrics for piecing
- 50" square of batting
- Navy and light gold embroidery floss
- Navy Pigma .05 pen
- Fusible web

CUTTING

1. From navy print fabric, cut the following borders: two each 5½" x 46½", 5½" x 36½", 2½" x 24½", 2½" x 20½", 1½" x 14½" and 1½" x 12½". Cut five 2½" x 44" strips for the binding.

2. From cream solid fabric, cut one 12½" square center block, four 5½" corner squares, and forty 3⅞" squares, cut diagonally for 80 triangles.

3. From one red print, tan homespun, blue plaid, and blue print fabrics, cut four 3⅜" squares each. Cut the squares diagonally.

4. From medium and dark scraps, cut two 3⅞" squares of each fabric for a total of 40 squares; cut the squares diagonally.

5. Refer to the General Instructions on page 6 to trace, apply fusible web to, and cut out the following appliqué shapes: One large heart, one medium heart, six corner flowers plus two center pieces for each flower, six extra large flowers plus a center for each,

14 large leaves, and four vine pieces (two and two reversed). For the vines, trace the patterns onto white paper, joining the pieces. Trace two vines from the front and two from the back of the paper to make right and left vines.

ASSEMBLY

1. Stitch two 1½" x 12½" navy borders to opposite sides of the center square. Add the two 1½" x 14½" borders to the top and bottom.

2. Place the square on the diagonal. Write the words "To have and to hold from this day forward" along the bottom edges of the cream block, using a navy Pigma pen. You may want to pencil in the words first, then darken the lines with the pen. Write the names of the bride and groom along the top edges. Embellish the writing as desired.

3. Center the two hearts on the cream block, and fuse in place. Blanket-stitch around the hearts using four strands of navy floss. Outline-stitch "Love" in the medium heart. With the Pigma pen, write the wedding date on both sides of the large heart.

4. Piece the four corner units as shown in Diagram A, and sew them to the center square. Layer and fuse a corner flower, black center, and tan homespun center in each corner block.

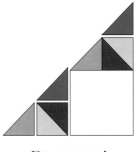

DIAGRAM A

Using floss, blanket-stitch around each appliqué piece.

5. Stitch a 2½" x 20½" border strip to the top and bottom of the center block, then add the 2½" x 24½" border strips to the sides.

6. Piece 80 bias-square units from the cream solid and medium and dark print and plaid fabrics. Sew the squares into four rows of eight squares each, and four rows of twelve squares each. Sew the rows together in pairs. Sew the shorter rows to the top and bottom of the center block, then sew the longer rows to the sides.

7. Add the 5½" x 36½" border strips to the top and bottom of the quilt top, then add the 5½" x 46½" border strips to the sides.

8. Referring to the photo, position and fuse the flowers, vines, and leaves on the borders. Blanket-stitch around all appliqué pieces using four strands of floss. Outline-stitch the stamens.

FINISHING

1. Press the completed top and take it to the wedding for the guests to sign, or mark quilting lines as desired. Refer to the General Instructions on page 7 to layer the wallhanging.

2. Quilt as desired. Trim the edges of the layers even. Prepare the binding strips and a hanging sleeve as directed on page 7. Sew the binding in place using a ¼" seam allowance; turn to the back and whipstitch in place.

MATERIALS

- ½ yard of cream solid fabric for cover
- ⅓ yard of navy print fabric for cording
- ⅛ yard each or scraps of red print, red homespun, blue plaid, and green homespun fabrics for appliqués
- Fusible web
- ½ yard of thin fleece
- 2 yards of 1/16" cording
- Navy and green embroidery floss
- Navy Pigma .05 pen
- Plain 10½" x 11⅝" photo album or three-ring binder
- Large sheet of plain paper

ASSEMBLY AND APPLIQUÉ

1. Open the album flat on a large sheet of paper; trace around the outside edges. Add a scant ¼" on all sides to allow for ease, plus an additional ½" seam allowance on the long sides and 1" on the short sides. Cut out the pattern.

2. Using the paper pattern, cut one layer of cream fabric and one piece of thin fleece. From the remaining cream fabric, cut two facing pieces the same height as the pattern but about 2"

shorter in width than the inside cover.

3. With the album open, measure along the top edge, down the front, and along the bottom edge. Cut the cording to this length, plus an extra inch or two. Cut enough 1½"-wide navy bias strips to cover the cording. Sew the strips together end to end to make one long strip. Using matching thread, cover the cording with the bias strip.

4. Using a ½" seam allowance, baste the cording to the right side of the cream fabric cover, aligning the raw edges. Begin at the back top corner, work along the top edge, around the front, and finally along the bottom edge. See Diagram B. Trim excess cording. Clip the seam allowance at the corners.

DIAGRAM B

5. Using a black permanent marker, write the words "Our Wedding Memories" and the couple's names on the pattern. Refer to the General Instructions on page 6 to trace, apply fusible web to, and cut out the following appliqué pieces: One large flower and flower center, two medium flowers and flower centers, three medium leaves, two small hearts, and two medium vines (one and one reversed).

6. Pin the cream fabric onto the paper pattern. Trace the lettering using the navy Pigma pen, embellishing the

writing as desired. Use a light box under the paper pattern if necessary. Position and fuse the appliqué shapes. If necessary, trim the horizontal vine slightly to fit the space.

7. Remove the paper pattern, and place the thin layer of fleece under the cream fabric. Stitch in place following the basting on the cording. Cut away the fleece from the seam allowances. Blanket-stitch the appliqués using three strands of floss.

8. Stitch a ¼" hem in one long side of each facing piece. Pin one facing piece to the right side of the cover, aligning the raw edges. Stitch in place, again following the previous stitching beside the cording. Trim the corners close to the stitching. Turn right side out and press.

9. Insert the album into the stitched end of the cover and check the fit; remove. Turn the cover inside out, pin the other facing piece in place, and baste. Turn right side out and slip the cover on the book again to check the fit. You may need to take a narrower or wider seam allowance. When pleased with the fit, stitch, and then trim the corners. Turn right side out and press. Insert the album into the cover.

5½" x 7½"

MATERIALS

- ⅓ yard of cream solid fabric for cover
- ¼ yard of navy print fabric for cording
- Scraps of red print, and red and green homespun fabrics for appliqués
- ¾ yard of ¹⁄₁₆" cording
- Scraps of fusible web
- ¼ yard of thin fleece
- Navy, green, and yellow embroidery floss
- ⅓ yard of ½"-wide satin ribbon
- One brass heart charm
- Navy Pigma .05 pen
- One large sheet of plain paper
- Plain 5½" x 7½" guest book

ASSEMBLY AND APPLIQUÉ

1. Follow the instructions for the Wedding Album, Steps 1 through 4, to create a paper pattern; cut the fabric and fleece, and add covered cording.

2. Using a black permanent marker, write the words "Guests of" and the couple's names onto the paper pattern. Refer to the General Instructions on page 6 to trace, apply fusible web to, and cut out the following appliqué pieces: Three small flowers, three small leaves, two small hearts, and two small vines (one and one reversed).

3. Pin the cream fabric onto the paper pattern. Trace the lettering using the navy Pigma pen. Use a light box under the pattern if necessary. Position and fuse the appliqué shapes. If necessary, trim the vertical vine to fit the space.

4. Remove the paper pattern, and place the thin layer of fleece under the cream fabric; stitch in place following the basted cording line. Cut away the fleece from the seam allowances. Blanket-stitch the appliqués using three strands of floss.

5. Stitch a ½" hem in one short side of each facing piece. Pin one piece to the right side of the cover, aligning the raw edges. Stitch in place, again following the stitching line on the cording. Trim the corners close to the stitching. Turn right side out and press.

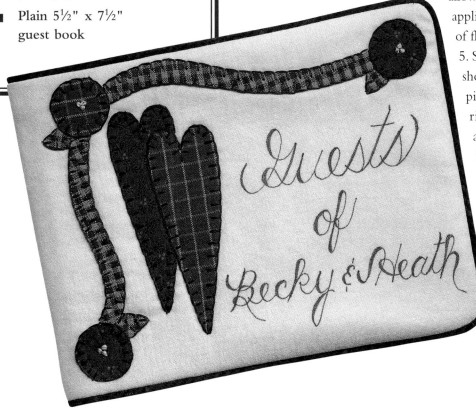

6. Insert the book into the stitched end of the cover and check for fit; remove. Turn the cover inside out, pin the other facing piece in place, and baste. Turn right side out and slip the cover on the book to check for fit; you may need to take a narrower or wider seam allowance. When you are pleased with the fit, stitch, and then trim the corners and turn right side out. Press. Insert the book into the completed cover.

7. Tack the ribbon to the inside top edge of the cover. Drape the ribbon over the book and determine the amount you want to extend from the bottom edge. Cut the ribbon and tie a knot at the end. Tack a brass heart at the knot.

Picture Frame

10" x 12"

MATERIALS

- ½ yard of navy fabric
- ¼ yard of red print fabric
- Scraps of red prints, cream plaid, and green homespun fabrics
- 10" x 12" piece of batting
- Scraps of fusible web
- Light gold embroidery floss
- 2 yards of ¹⁄₁₆" cording
- Three pieces of mat board, two 10" x 12" and one 4" x 9"
- Hot-glue gun and glue sticks or white fabric glue
- X-Acto knife or utility knife
- Spray adhesive

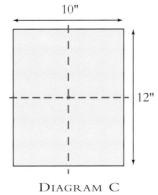

DIAGRAM C

1. Find the center of one large mat board as shown in Diagram C, and mark lines with a pencil. Cut out a 3" x 5" paper pattern for the frame opening (larger if desired). Fold the paper in half both ways and crease. Open up, and align the creases on the paper pattern with the lines on the mat. Trace around the paper. Cut out the opening on the traced lines.

2. Lay the mat board on the batting, trace around the inside of the opening, and cut on the traced lines.

3. Apply spray adhesive to the front of the mat board. Center the mat on the batting, adhesive side down, and press.

4. Cut two 12" x 14" pieces from navy fabric. Center the mat board on the wrong side of one piece, leaving 1" of fabric showing on all sides; trace the opening; remove. Cut ½" inside the traced lines, and clip the fabric almost to the corners.

5. Refer to the General Directions on page 6 to trace, apply fusible web to, and cut out one large flower and flower center, three medium leaves, and two small hearts. Position and fuse the appliqué pieces to the fabric, using the photograph on page 135 as a guide to placement. Blanket-stitch around the appliqués using three strands of floss. Press the stitched fabric front.

6. Center the mat board, batting-side down, on the wrong side of the stitched fabric. Bring the fabric in the opening toward the back; glue the top and bottom edges in place first, then the sides. Fold the outside edges to the back and glue.

7. Cut enough 1½"-wide red bias strips to cover 72" of cording. Stitch the

strips together end to end to make one long strip. Using matching thread, cover the cording with the bias strip.

8. Cut two 3½" and two 5½" pieces of covered cording. Glue the 3½" pieces to the inside top and bottom of the picture opening and the 5½" strips to the sides. Let dry.

9. Glue the remaining cording along the outside edges, beginning at the center bottom edge, clipping the seam allowance at the corners and overlapping the ends.

10. For the frame back, cover the remaining large mat board in the same manner as the front, omitting the opening. Cut one 9½" x 11½" piece of navy fabric, and glue to the remaining (inside) surface of the frame back.

11. Place the frame front on the back and glue the sides and bottom together, leaving the top open to insert a photo.

12. Referring to Diagram D, make an easel from the 4" x 9" mat board. Mark the shape on the board as shown, and mark a score line 1" down from the top so that the easel can bend. Cut out the shape, and score the board along the line, being careful not to cut all the way through the mat. Cover with navy fabric and glue the edges. Fold on the score line. Center the easel on the frame back, aligning the bottom edge with the bottom of the frame. Glue the top, above the fold, to the frame back. Insert the picture from the top of the frame.

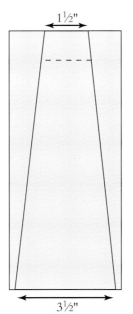

1½"

3½"

DIAGRAM D

10" x 7" x 5"

MATERIALS

- ¾ yard each of navy print and red homespun fabrics for box and box lining
- ¼ yard of red print fabric for box lid and cording
- Scraps of red print, cream solid, and tan homespun fabrics for box lid
- ½ yard of fusible fleece
- Scrap of fusible web
- Navy embroidery floss
- ½ yard of ⅛"-wide red satin ribbon
- Navy quilting thread
- ¾ yard of ¹⁄₁₆" cording
- 15" x 20" piece of cardboard
- Navy Pigma .05 pen
- 3 brass heart charms in various sizes
- Fabric glue

CUTTING

1. From the navy print fabric, cut two 6½" x 1½" strips and two 3½" x 1½" strips for the patchwork top.

2. From the red homespun fabric, cut two 6½" x 1½" and two 3½" x 1½" strips, and two 2" squares cut diagonally.

3. From the cream solid fabric, cut one 3½" x 6½" rectangle. From the tan homespun, cut two 2" squares and cut these diagonally.

4. Refer to the General Instructions on

"Two souls in one" and "Two hearts into one heart" onto white paper. Pin the patchwork top onto the paper with the cream fabric over the lettering. Place the heart appliqué in position and fuse. Trace the lettering using the navy Pigma pen, embellishing your writing as desired. Remove the paper pattern. Blanket-stitch around the heart using two strands of navy floss. Press the top.

3. Following the manufacturer's directions, adhere the fusible fleece pieces to the wrong side of the navy print and red homespun fabrics, allowing 1" to 2" between the pieces. On the patchwork top, you will have only $\frac{1}{2}$" seam allowance on all edges. Cut out the pieces, adding a $\frac{1}{2}$" fabric margin on all edges.

4. Pin a navy and a red 5" x 7" side piece right sides together; machine-stitch together along one long and two short edges, sewing right next to the fleece edges. Turn right side out. Baste the unstitched edge closed. Repeat for the other side piece, and the front and back pieces. Sew all four sides of the bottom piece, leaving an opening for turning; turn right side out and sew the opening closed. Set aside the top.

5. Pin a 5" x 7" side piece to the bottom piece, navy sides together, matching the closed edges. Using navy quilting thread, whipstitch the pieces together, catching all layers. Repeat with the remaining side and front and back pieces. Now stitch the 5" sides together to form the box. Turn the box right side (navy side) out.

6. Remove the basting stitches from the top edges of all four sides and slip the cardboard pieces between the fabric layers. Turn the seam allowances in and blind-stitch the top edges closed.

page 6 to trace, apply fusible web to, and cut the memory box heart pattern on page 142 from a scrap of red print.

5. From the fusible fleece, cut four 7" x 10" pieces for the tops and bottoms, four 5" x 10" pieces for the front and back, and four 5" x 7" sides. You will cut the corresponding fabric pieces later.

6. From the cardboard, cut two $6\frac{1}{2}$" x $9\frac{1}{2}$" pieces for the top and bottom, two $4\frac{1}{2}$" x $9\frac{1}{2}$" pieces for the front and back, and two $4\frac{1}{2}$" x $6\frac{1}{2}$" pieces for the sides.

ASSEMBLY

1. To piece the patchwork top, place the $1\frac{1}{2}$" red and navy strips right sides together in pairs, and sew with a $\frac{1}{2}$" seam allowance. Sew the red and tan homespun triangles together into squares. Sew the squares to the ends of the $6\frac{1}{2}$" strips, referring to the photo as needed for correct color placement. Sew the $3\frac{1}{2}$" strips to the short sides of the cream rectangle. Join the three rows as shown in Diagram F.

2. Using a black marker, trace the heart from page 142 and write the words

DIAGRAM F

7. Cut enough $1\frac{1}{2}$"-wide red bias strips to cover 27" of cording. Sew the strips together end to end to make one long strip. Using matching thread, cover the cording with the bias strip.

8. Using a $\frac{1}{2}$" seam allowance, baste the cording to the wrong side of the patchwork top, starting at the back corner on a 7" side, working across the front and along the other side; tuck in the raw ends.

9. Cut three 9" pieces of ribbon. Thread a brass heart charm onto each piece and tie a knot at the end of each ribbon. Tie all three ribbons together at the opposite end, letting the hearts hang at various lengths. Center and pin the knotted end of the ribbons to the wrong side of the patchwork top.

10. Pin the patchwork top and the lid lining wrong sides together, and blindstitch the corded edges, allowing the ribbons to dangle away from the lid.

11. Slip a $6\frac{1}{2}$" x $9\frac{1}{2}$" cardboard between the patchwork top and the red lining. Baste the back edge, then place this edge of the lid along the back of the box, right sides together. Pin and then whipstitch in place.

12. Cut an 8" x 11" piece of the lining fabric to cover the $6\frac{1}{2}$" x $9\frac{1}{2}$" bottom cardboard piece. Bring the cut edges to the back of the cardboard and glue in place. Set this covered piece into the bottom of the box.

BALL JAR SCRUNCHY

Here's a clever way to turn a simple canning jar into a charming vase—add a scrunchy! Cut a $3\frac{1}{4}$" x 16" strip of navy fabric. Hem the short ends, then fold the strip lengthwise, right sides together, and stitch with a $\frac{1}{4}$" seam allowance. Turn right side out and press. Insert a $1\frac{1}{4}$" x 12" piece of elastic into the tube, bring the ends together and stitch. Pull the fabric ends together and blindstitch. Trace, apply fusible web to, and cut out assorted flowers and matching centers. Fuse each flower to the wrong side of a matching flower, inserting the end of a piece of wire about 7" long between the layers before fusing. Fuse a flower center in place. Tie a narrow strip of green homespun around each wire below the flower. Gather the stems as you would a bouquet, wrap them together with another wire, and cut the ends even. Whipstitch to the inside of the scrunchy. Cut a $\frac{1}{2}$" x 16" strip of green homespun and tie into a bow. Hot glue the bow at the top edge of the scrunchy, just below the flower stems. Place the scrunchy around a $12\frac{1}{2}$" diameter Ball jar and fill the jar with your favorite wildflowers.

Suellen Wassem

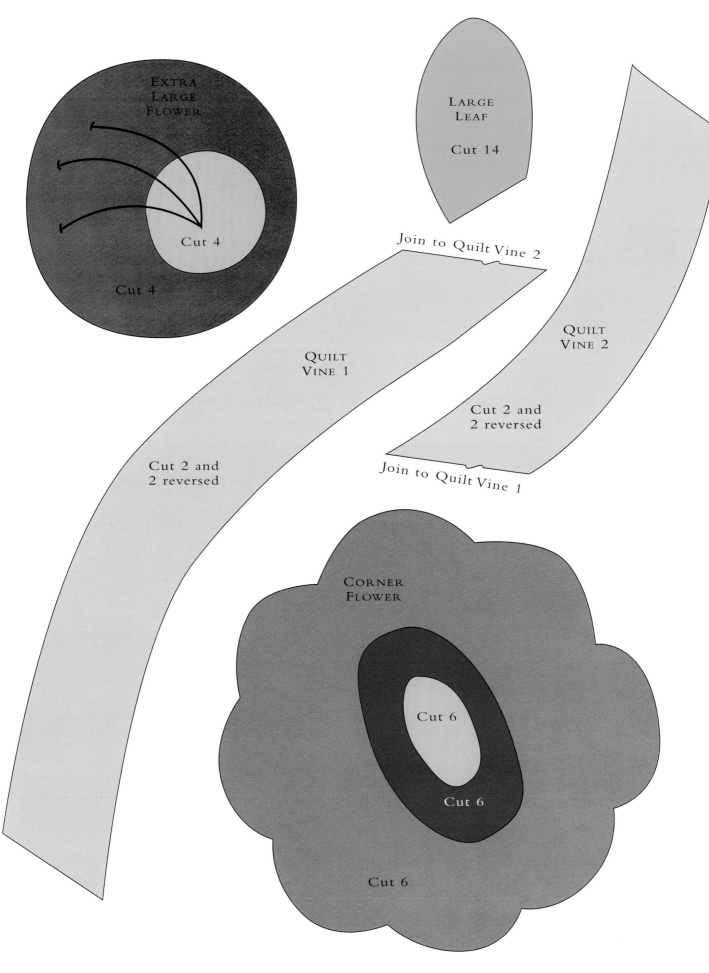

EXTRA
LARGE
FLOWER

Cut 4

Cut 4

LARGE
LEAF

Cut 14

Join to Quilt Vine 2

QUILT
VINE 1

QUILT
VINE 2

Cut 2 and
2 reversed

Join to Quilt Vine 1

Cut 2 and
2 reversed

CORNER
FLOWER

Cut 6

Cut 6

Cut 6

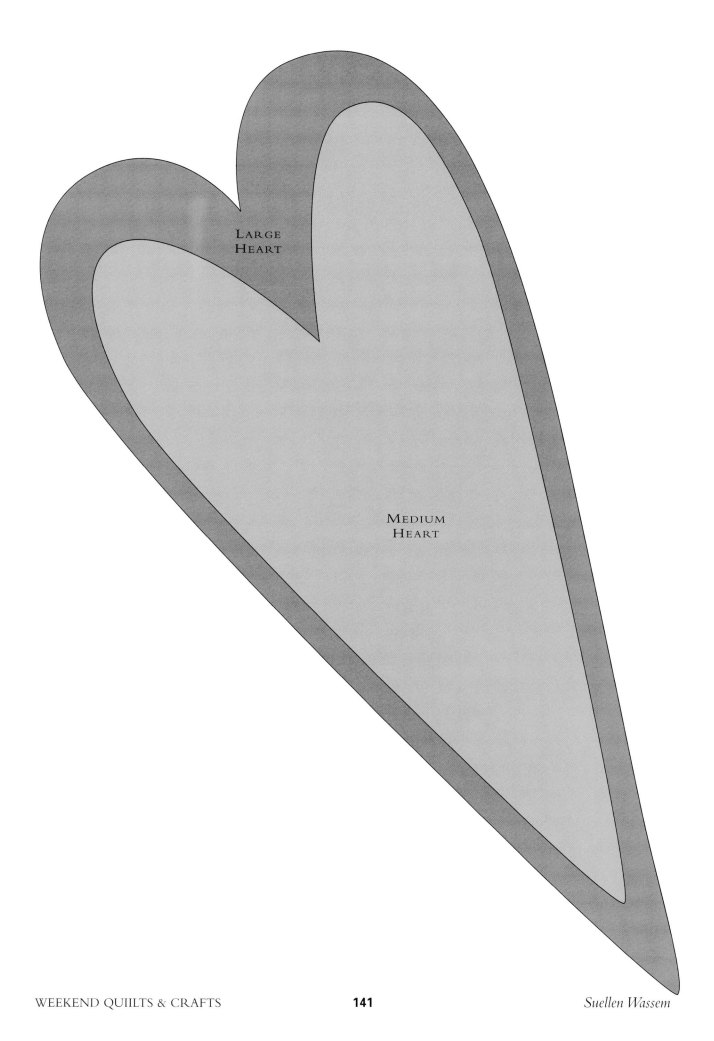

Large
Heart

Medium
Heart

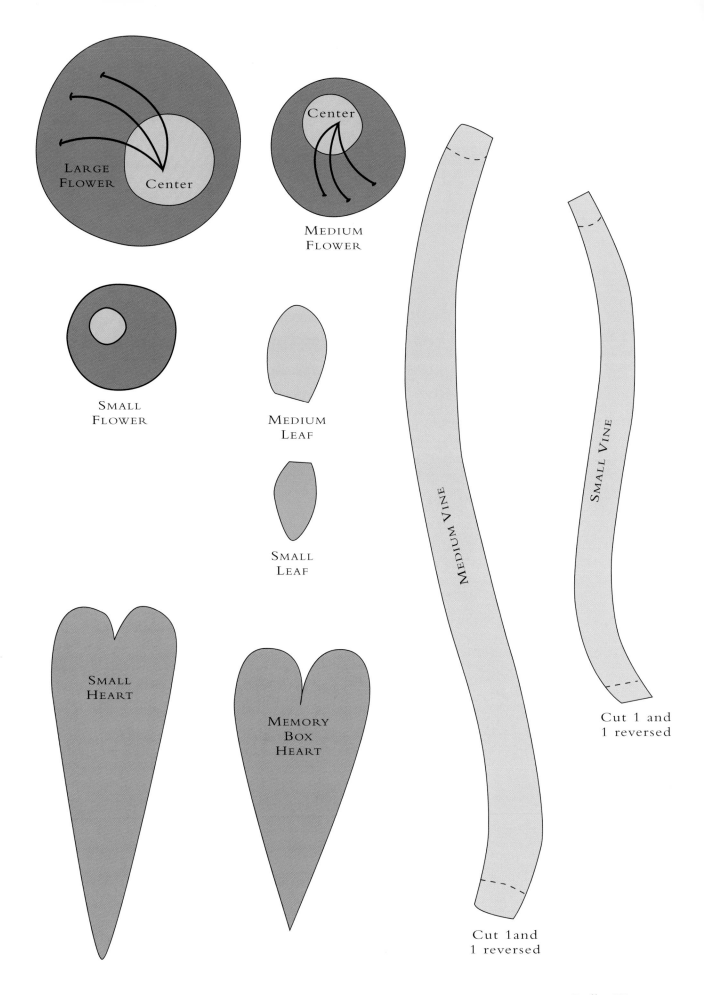

LARGE
FLOWER

Center

Center

MEDIUM
FLOWER

SMALL
FLOWER

MEDIUM
LEAF

SMALL
LEAF

MEDIUM VINE

SMALL VINE

Cut 1 and
1 reversed

SMALL
HEART

MEMORY
BOX
HEART

Cut 1and
1 reversed

TIPS & TECHNIQUES

TEA-STAINING FABRIC

Let eight teabags steep in 3 cups of boiling water until cool. Place the fabric in the tea solution and soak 1/3 to 3 hours, depending on the desired depth of fabric.

To stain a project, after sewing and stuffing is completed, apply the tea solution with a cotton ball, rag, or paper towel, making sure to work the solution into the seams.

SEWING-ON BUTTONS

For a decorative finish, use three strands of embroidery floss to sew buttons onto quilts and projects. Do not knot the end of the floss. Sew down through one button hole to back of quilt and up through second hole. Tie floss tails into a knot on top of the button. Apply a dot of clear-drying glue on the knot and clip the floss tails.

USING A HOT GLUE GUN

When shopping for a hot glue gun look for one with a trigger mechanism for dispersing the hot glue, and with dual temperature controls (or purchse two guns).

Guns come in two sizes: The large size covers large areas quickly; the small size works great on craft projects that require precision placement of glue.

Low temperature glue (wax sticks) melts at a lower temperature and is easier to work with, but one caution—the heat of outdoors, a sunny window, or a hot attic (where Christmas decorations are most often stored) can melt the glue, too.

CLEANING EMBELLISHED CLOTHING

Hand-wash your fused garment, or turn it inside-out and wash with cold water in the washing machine on the delicate cycle. Line-dry or dry flat. If fused pieces start to lift, use an iron to press them back into place. You may need to place a piece of fusible web under the edge to re-adhere.

Use lightweight fusible web if you will be machine-washing and drying your garment. If the fabric is stretchy, place a tear-away stabilizer on the inside of the garment, under the design area; machine-appliqué around pieces to secure them to the fabric.

Robyn Pandolph

SENTIMENTAL JOURNEY

When Robyn Pandolph was a busy, stay-at-home mother of four, little did she dream that her future held a career as a nationally recognized fabric designer, quilting teacher, and author.

In 1993, when her children were more independent, Robyn decided to take some time for herself and learn to quilt. She joined the Lakeview Quilting Guild and started making up her own folk art style designs. From that small beginning, she was asked to teach in a local quilt shop. The more Robyn taught, the more she was asked to design. Within a year she launched a new idea, the Folk Art Angel Appliqué Block of the Month.

Shortly thereafter Robyn took the program to the International Quilt Market in Houston, and subsequently launched her own pattern company and home decorating fabric lines such as Sentimental Journey for South Sea Imports. Robyn's signature look is a sophisticated blend of romantic pastel colors and nineteenth century chintzes and decorator fabrics.

Robyn's Sentimental Journey collection featured on the following pages includes a wall hanging, garment bag, sewing box, and needle cases—perfect gifts for a recent graduate or bride!

MATERIALS

- 1¼ yards of lavender print fabric
- 1 yard plaid fabric
- ⅛ yard of stripe fabric
- 1⅜ yards lavender floral fabric
- One 7" square of pink wool felt
- One 4" square of green wool felt
- Two pink buttons
- 6 yards of lavender ⅝" grosgrain ribbon
- 5 yards of ¼" cording for piping
- One 8" x 24" piece of batting
- One large brass hanger

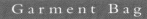

Garment Bag

CUTTING

1. From lavender print fabric, cut three strips 1¾" x 43" for piping, one 8" x 24" rectangle for upper front, and two pieces 12½" x 43" for lining the inside lower front.

2. From plaid fabric, cut one 5" x 44" bias rectangle, for ruffle

3. From stripe fabric, cut one 1¾" x 24" rectangle for piping.

4. From lavender floral fabric, cut two pieces 23" x 43" for the back and two pieces 23" x 36" for the front.

5. From the pink felt, cut the heart using a pinking rotary blade (pattern on page 153—same heart as wallhanging).

6. From the green felt, cut the four leaves. (pattern on page 153).

ASSEMBLY

1. Place the 8" x 24" piece of batting under the lavender print of the same size. Quilt a diagonal grid with the lines spaced 2" apart.

2. Place the brass hanger on the quilted fabric and trace around the top curves adding a ½" seam allowance.

145 *Robyn Pandolph*

3. Monogram the heart, if you wish. Stitch the heart and leaves to the top front, using the sewing machine. With thread that matches the buttons, sew the buttons in place as shown in the picture.

4. For the piping, lay the cord for the center of the wrong side of the 1¾" x 24" stripe fabric rectangle. Fold and pin the fabric over the cord, with the raw edges even. Using a zipper foot, sew close to the cord along the length of the strip. Trim so there is ¼" seam allowance.

5. Align the raw edge of the piping and the lower edge of the quilted front piece. Using a zipper foot and a basting stitch, baste the piping in place.

6. With wrong sides together, sew the edges of the plaid bias strip together using a basting stitch. (Leave enough thread at the beginning and the end to make gathering easy.) Stitch again, stitching just inside the first row of stitches. To gather, pull the two top threads to 23 inches.

7. With right sides together, sew one 23" x 36" piece of lavender floral lining fabric to one 23" x 36" piece of

lavender floral fabric. Using a ¼" seam allowance, sew along one side for 36 inches. Turn with wrong sides together and press. Repeat for the other side.

8. Cut eight 12½" pieces of grosgrain ribbon for ties. Pin lavender grosgrain ribbon to each finished side with the lavender floral on the outside, leaving approximately ⅛" of the lavender floral showing. Place ties under ribbon, starting four inches from the top and space approximately nine inches apart. Topstitch on both sides of the ribbon. Fold over tie and bartack. Tie a knot in the end of each tie.

9. Abutting the two top edges, stitch together using a wide zigzag stitch. Repeat at the bottom opening.

10. With the right side of the lower front section and the right side of the upper front section together, pin in place. Stitch the seam with the zipper foot to ensure stitching close to the piping.

11. Using the front pattern as your guide, cut two back pieces on the 23" x 43" piece of lavender floral. One will be used for the lining.

12. Sew together the three 1½" strips of lavender print to make the piping strip for the outside edge. Follow the directions from Step 4 for making the piping. Stitch to the edges of the front in the same manner as described in Step 5. Round the bottom two corners.

13. Lay back and lining with wrong sides together, for one piece. Place the front and back together with right sides together and pin. Starting approximately an inch from the top middle, stitch the front to the back, following the basting lines used to

attach the piping. Stop about one inch from the top center. This allows for an opening for the hanger. Turn right side out.

14. Wrap one yard of lavender grosgrain ribbon around the throat of the hanger and tie a bow.

Tote Bag

MATERIALS

- One 4½" square of yellow paisley fabric
- ⅓ yard of small yellow flowered print
- ⅛ yard blue flowered fabric
- ¼ yard pink flowered fabric
- ⅛ yard deep rose print fabric for piping
- ⅔ yard yellow stripe for back and sides of tote
- 1½ yards pink fabric for lining
- Deep rose and gold embroidery floss
- 1 yard 1" dark pink grosgrain ribbon
- Batting
- 4 yards ⅝" piping

CUTTING

1. Cut one 4½" square of yellow paisley fabric.

2. From blue floral fabric, cut thirty-six 3" squares and two 3¾" squares. Cut the two 3¾" squares diagonally for four triangles.

3. From yellow flowered print fabric, cut two 4⅞" squares. Cut each square diagonally for four triangles.

ASSEMBLY—
STEP 1

ASSEMBLY—
STEP 2

ASSEMBLY—
STEP 3

ASSEMBLY—
STEP 3

ASSEMBLY—
STEP 4

4. From yellow flowered print fabric, cut four 4½" squares and four 4½" x 8½" rectangles.

5. From pink floral fabric, cut two 2½" x 16½" rectangles for the handles and eight 4½" squares.

6. From deep rose fabric, cut four 1½" x 42" strips of fabric.

7. From yellow stripe, cut one 4½" x 42" rectangle for the sides of the tote, and one 4½" x 6" rectangle and one 16½" square for the back of the tote.

ASSEMBLY

1. Sew blue flowered triangles to opposite sides of the 4½" yellow paisley square. Press toward the triangles. Sew triangles to the remaining two sides. Press.

2. Sew yellow flowered print triangles to the sides of the newly formed square in the manner described in Step 1.

3. Place 4½" pink floral squares to the left side of four 4½" x 8½" yellow flowered print rectangles. Draw a diagonal line corner to corner and sew on line. Cut away ½" from the sew line and press toward the triangle. Repeat for the remaining sides.

4. Following the diagram, sew 4½" yellow flowered print squares to the ends of two of the units and sew two units to opposite sides of the square unit.

5. Sew the three units together to form a star.

6. Following instructions on page 7, fuse a blue flowered heart to the center of the yellow paisley square. Using deep rose floss, stitch around the heart with a buttonhole stitch.

7. Cut a piece of batting the size of the front of the tote bag. Pin the two layers together and quilt the layers by stitching in the ditch.

8. With gold floss, tie corners of the inside square.

9. Diagonally piece the four deep rose fabric $1\frac{1}{2}$" x 42" strips. Lay the piping in the center of the wrong side of the deep rose fabric strip. Fold and pin the fabric over the cord, with the raw edges even. Using a zipper foot, sew close to the cord along the length of the strip. Trim so there is a $\frac{1}{4}$" seam allowance.

10. Pin piping to the sides and bottom of the tote front by aligning the raw edges of the piping to edge of the quilted block. Clip the edge to make a corner. Using a zipper foot and a basting stitch, baste the piping in place.

11. Stitch the two $4\frac{1}{2}$" pieces of yellow stripe fabric together for the sides of the tote. Back the piece with batting and quilt the $4\frac{1}{2}$" width with a straight line approximately every three inches.

12. With right sides together, pin the side piece to the tote front. Using a zipper foot and following the basting line, sew the two pieces together.

13. Place a $16\frac{1}{2}$" square of batting under the $16\frac{1}{2}$" yellow striped square. Quilt following the straight lines of the stripe approximately every two inches. Apply piping to the sides and bottoms following the procedure used in Step 10. Sew the back to the sides following the procedure in Step 12.

14. Following the procedure in Step 10, sew piping to the top edge of the tote.

15. Fold the blue flowered 3" squares in half twice to make prairie points

16. Following the layout on page 147, pin the prairie points over the bias strip. With right sides facing, align long raw edge of each prairie point with raw edge of top. Slip folded edge of triangle (prairie point) into open side of each adjacent triangle so that they overlap slightly. Baste in place.

17. To make the handles, fold each $2\frac{1}{2}$" x $16\frac{1}{2}$" pink floral fabric rectangles over a 1" x $16\frac{1}{2}$" piece of batting. Stitch down the center. Lay the dark pink 1" grosgrain ribbon on the unfinished edge. Stitch on both sides of the ribbon. Place edge of straps 3" from the center and baste in place.

18. Cut the pink lining fabric into two $16\frac{1}{2}$" squares and a $4\frac{1}{2}$" x $47\frac{1}{2}$" strip. Using Steps 11–13, sew together, elimanting the piping. Leave an opening for turning the bag.

19. Place the tote lining inside the outer part with right sides together. Pin and then stitch using a zipper foot.

20. Turn inside out through the opening in the lining. Hand-stitch the opening closed.

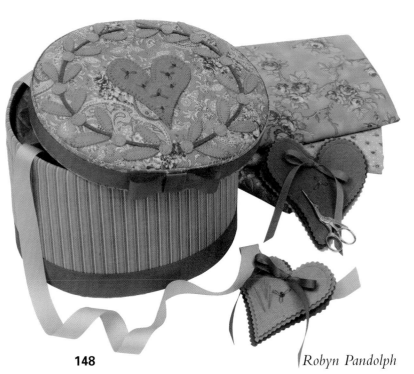

MATERIALS

- Oval cardboard craft box: circumference 31½", height 7½; (or size of your choice)
- 1 yard of 1½" pink grosgrain ribbon
- 1½" yard of 1" pink grosgrain ribbon
- 12" square of green wool felt
- 6" square of pink, light green, and dark green wool felt

NOTE: If you want to soften the colors of the felt, you may tea-dye it.

- ½ yard of pink paisley print
- ⅓ yard of blue striped fabric
- Raspberry, teal and green embroidery floss
- 16" square and 7½" x 32" piece of lightweight batting
- 12" square of white felt
- Photo-mount spray adhesive
- Template plastic

CUTTING

1. Trace appliqué of leaf and berry on page 155 pattern onto Template plastic. Trace twenty-four leaves onto light green wool felt and cut out. Trace twelve berries onto pink wool felt and cut. Cut a ⅜" x 12" strip of dark green wool felt.

2. Straight line and Buttonhole stitch leaves and berries to a 14" x 16" pink paisley rectangle using the photograph as a guide. With green embroidery floss, make seven flowers using the

LAZY-DAISY STITCH

FRENCH KNOT

BUTTONHOLE

STRAIGHT STITCH

lazy-daisy stitch. With raspberry floss, stitch three French knots to make the centers of the flowers.

3. Trim pink paisley rectangle with appliqué the size of the oval lid plus one inch and one 3" x 33" rectangle.

4. Trace the top of box on batting and cut following traced line.

5. From the blue striped fabric, cut a 9½" x 33" rectangle.

6. Trim pink paisley rectangle with appliqué, cut one piece the size of the oval lid plus one inch and one 3" x 33" rectangle.

7. From the 1" pink grosgrain ribbon, cut 34 inches, one piece 10 inches, and one piece two inches.

8. From the 1½" pink grosgrain ribbon, cut one piece 34 inches.

9. From traced pattern of box, cut felt about ¼" smaller than the pattern with a rotary pinking blade if you have one.

ASSEMBLY

1. Using spray adhesive the 7½" x 32" piece of batting to the sides of the box. Trim so that the batting meets and does not overlap.

2. Spray the 9½" x 33" blue striped rectangle with adhesive and apply to the sides of the box. Turn under and overlap where the edges come together, fold over top of box and turn down about one inch. Clip the bottom and glue around.

3. Using adhesive spray, attach the white felt to the bottom of the box.

4. Bring 1½" pink grosgrain ribbon around box to determine exact size, overlap, turn ends under, remove, and whipstitch the seam. Slip back on coming up from the bottom, aligning the seam with the blue strip fabric. seam. Make a small stitch to secure.

5. With green embroidery floss, make seven flowers using the lazy-daisy stitch. With raspberry floss, stitch three French Knots to make the centers of the flowers.

6. With spray adhesive, attach the batting to the lid and then attach the appliquéd piece in the same manner.

7. Press under ¼" on the long side of the 3" x 33" pink paisley rectangle and then attacfh to the rim of the lid with spray adhesive. The excess will be brought to the inside of the lid.

8. Turn under and overlap the 1" grosgrain ribbon and whipstitch in place. Put it on the rim of the lid, and using the 10" and 12" pieces, make a bow and attach it over the seam.

Needle Case and Scissors Case

MATERIALS

- 7" square of wool felt in three colors for scissors case
- 6" square of wool felt in cream and three other colors for scissors case
- Rotary cutter with pinking blade
- Green, pink and raspberry embroidery floss
- 40" square of batting
- 22" of ³⁄₈" pink grosgrain ribbon
- 22" of ³⁄₈" blue grosgrain ribbon

CUTTING

1. For the needle case, trace the pattern for three hearts (page 154) on Template plastic. Draw the line onto pink, light green and dark green wool felt. Cut out on drawn line using the rotary pinking blade. Cut a cream-colored heart the same size as the small heart, using a straight edge scissors.

2. For the scissors case, follow the same procedure in Step 1, using the heart patterns on page 154. Also cut the scissors holder with a pinking blade.

ASSEMBLY

1. For the needle case, on the smallest heart about an inch below the center of the top, make three lazy-daisy stitches using green floss and three French knots using bright pink floss. Center the smallest heart on top of the medium heart. Pin the layers together, and machine-stitch inside the outside edge of the small heart. Center the small cream-colored heart on the large heart, and stitch down the center of the heart. Layer the hearts, and punch two holes through all layers just below the inside point on the top heart. Take the grosgrain ribbon through from the top and back through to the top. Tie a bow.

2. For the scissors case, follow the procedure from Step 1, except machine-stitch the scissors holder to the large heart, leaving the top open.

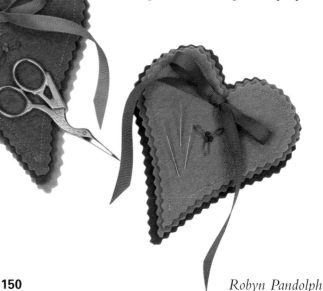

Finished size 36" square

MATERIALS

- ⅞ yard of gold fabric for block background
- ½ yard pink flowered fabric for sashing
- ⅓ yard blue flowered fabric for inside border and appliqué
- ¾ yard pink paisley fabric for outer border
- ⅞ yard yellow flowered fabric ror outside border and binding
- ⅛ yard green flowered fabric for appliqué
- 40" square of fabric for backing
- 40" square of batting
- 1 yard of fusible web

CUTTING

1. From gold fabric, cut four 13" square.
2. From pink flowered fabric, cut two 1" x 12½" rectangles, two 1" x 25" rectangles, and two 1" x 26" rectangles.
3. From blue flowered fabric, cut two 2¾" x 26" rectangles and two 2¾" x 30½" rectangles for inner border.
4. From pink paisley fabric, cut forty 3½" squares for outer border.
5. From yellow flowered fabric, cut four 3½" squares, thirty 3½" x 6½" rectangles, for the outer border. Cut four 2½" x 42" strips for the binding.

ASSEMBLY

1. Prepare the four appliquéd blocks. From the pattern on page 155, trace the hearts, stems, and leaves onto fusible web. For fusing instructions, ferer to General Instructions on page 6. Fuse the leaves and stems to the green flowered fabric, the bow to the blue flowered fabric, and the hearts to the pink flowered fabric. Refer to the pattern on page 155 for placement and fuse pattern pieces onto the gold background squares. The blocks will be trimmed to $12\frac{1}{2}$" after the appliqué is finished, so be sure to stay within the 12" finished size of the block.

2. Using a satin stitch, appliqué the pieces to the background using matching thread. Trim the blocks to $12\frac{1}{2}$".

3. For each row, join two appliquéd blocks with a 1" x $12\frac{1}{2}$" rectangle, press toward the sashing.

4. Join the two rows by sewing a 1" x 26" pink flowered fabric rectangle between them. Press

ASSEMBLY—
STEP 7

ASSEMBLY—
STEP 7

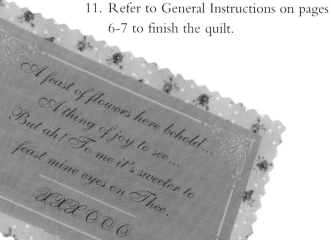

ASSEMBLY—
STEP 7

toward the sashing. Sew two 1" x 25" rectangles to top and bottom of piece, and two 1" x 26" rectangles to the sides. Press.

5. Sew the two $2\frac{3}{4}$" x 26" blue flowered fabric rectangles to the top and bottom of the quilt. Press toward the border.

6. Sew the two $2\frac{3}{4}$" x $30\frac{1}{2}$" blue flowered fabric rectangles to the sides of the quilt. Press.

7. Place twenty $3\frac{1}{2}$" pink paisley squares to the left side of sixteen $3\frac{1}{2}$" x $6\frac{1}{2}$" yellow flowered fabric rectangles and four $3\frac{1}{2}$" x $6\frac{1}{2}$" yellow flowered fabric rectangles. Draw a diagonal line corner to corner. Sew on line. Cut away $\frac{1}{4}$" from sewn line, press toward triangle. Trim Repeat for the remaining side.

8. Sew 5 units together for each side using the photograph as a guide.

9. Sew one border unit to the top and one unit to the bottom of the quilt.

10. Sew a $3\frac{1}{2}$" yellow square to each end of the remaining two units. Then attach these units to the sides of the quilt.

11. Refer to General Instructions on pages 6-7 to finish the quilt.

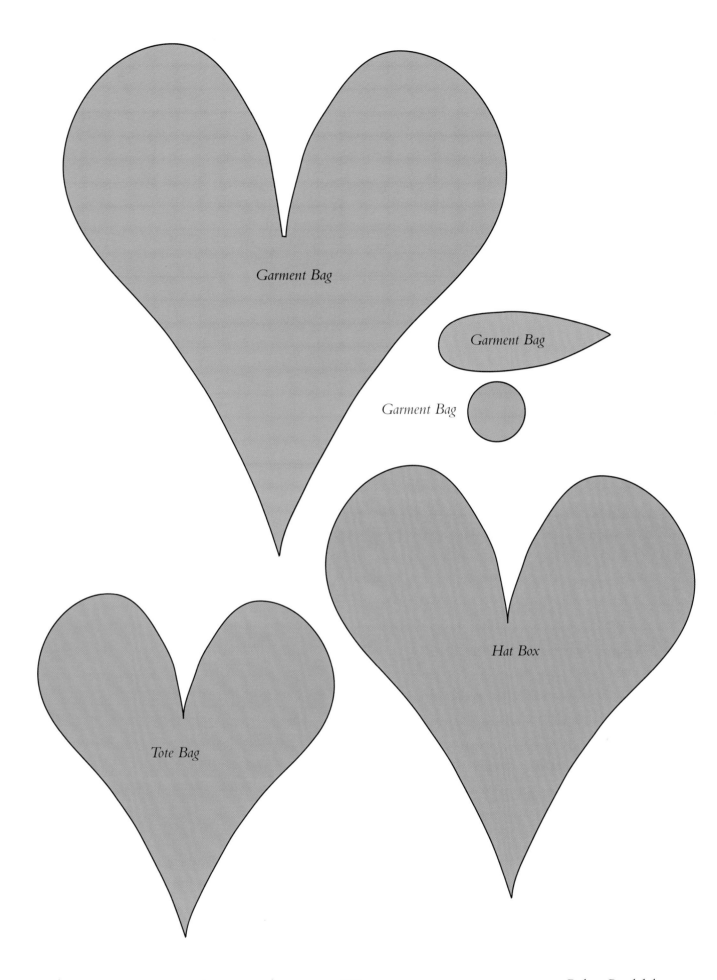

Garment Bag

Garment Bag

Garment Bag

Hat Box

Tote Bag

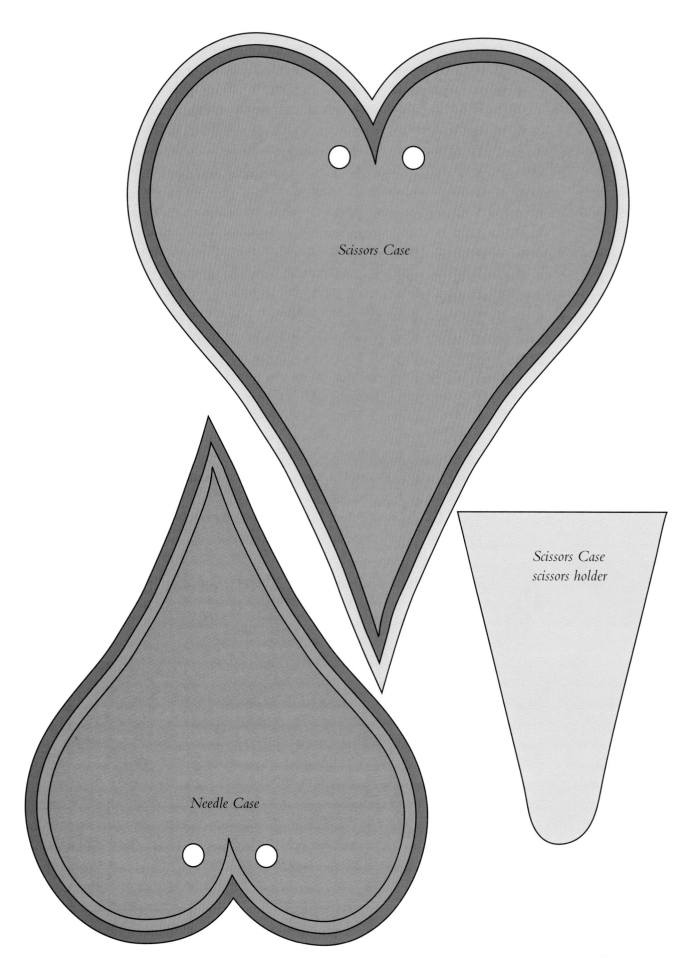

Scissors Case

Scissors Case
scissors holder

Needle Case

Enlarge 150%

Retta Warehime

HEART 'N HOME

Some evenings Retta Warehime stays up well past 2:00 am sewing and creating. She is a dedicated quilter who loves her job. Working from home allows Retta the flexible schedule often required by creative people.

Retta was introduced to quilting by her friends Jackie Wolff, Debbie Mumm, and Ann Weisbeck in Spokane, Washington. In the 24 years that Retta has been quilting she keeps busy designing, teaching, and writing through her company Sew Cherished. Retta is the author of several books and has also published original designs for several quilting magazines.

Retta has four children and three grandchildren. In addition, she and her husband host two WHL hockey players who live in their home eight months out of the year. Despite her hectic family life, Retta makes as many as 40 quilts a year. Designing and quilting soothes her soul. Retta's greatest pleasure is making quilts for others and donating quilts to charity auctions to benefit children and cancer patients.

The Heart 'n Home wallhanging was "borrowed" for photography from friend Jane Loh of Sammamish, Washington who has received this quilted keepsake as a gift from Retta's generous heart. The other projects in the collection are a permanent part of Retta's home and offer warmth and charm to her friends and family.

MATERIALS

- ½ yard of tan print for background
- ⅜ yard of tan for center
- ¼ yard of red small print for inside border
- 1 yard of dark blue print for outer border
- ⅓" yard for binding
- ⅜ yard of flannel for backing for the lettered panel
- ⅛ yard each of six darks, medium darks, and lights or scraps for four heart and four home blocks
- 1¼ yards for backing
- 45" square for batting
- Black and red embroidery floss

Heart 'n Home Wallhanging

Finished size 41" square

CUTTING

1. From the background, cut two 2" x 33½" strips, two 2" x 30½" strips, four 1½" x 10½" rectangles, four 1½" x 9½" rectangles, two 1" x 10½" rectangles, and two 1" x 9½" rectangles.

2. From the red small print inner border fabric, cut two 1½" x 35½" strips two 1½" x 33½" strips.

3. From the dark blue outer border print, cut two 3½" x 41½" strips two 3½" x 35½" strips.

4. From the tan center fabric, cut one 13" square, and from the flannel, cut one 13" square.

5. Follow the cutting instructions for the house, and cut enough pieces for four houses.

6. Follow the cutting instructions for the heart, and cut enough pieces for four hearts.

Where friendships are formed
And families are grown
Where joy is shared
And true love is known
Where memories are made
And quilts are sewn
This is a place
Called heart and home ♡

Where memories are made
And quilts are sewn
This is a place
Called heart and home
♡ ♡ ♡ ♡ ♡ ♡

ASSEMBLY

1. Sew four heart blocks (directions on page 161) and four house blocks (directions on page 160).

2. Center and lightly trace all words on page 00, with a fabric pencil on the 13" square piece of tan fabric. This piece of fabric will be cut down to a 9½" square, so center before tracing.

3. Press the flannel and center square piece (right side up) together. Baste layers together for stitching or put in a hoop.

4. Using a backstitch, two strands of black floss and small stitches, a little less than ⅛", embroider the saying.

5. Embroider the hearts with two strands of red floss. Press the block flat. If you use steam, test the floss for color fastness before pressing.

6. Make sure the words are centered, and then trim down to a 9½" square.

7. Sew the 1" x 9½" background strips to the top and bottom of the lettered panel and the 1" x 10½" background strips to each side.

8. Sew a 1½" x 9½" background strip to the top of TWO houses and only the bottom of TWO houses.

9. Sew a 1½" x 10½" background strip on the right side of one house with strip on top and on one house with strip on bottom.

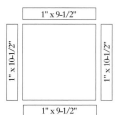

STEP 7

STEP 8

10. Sew a 1½" x 10½" background strip on the left side of one house with strip on top and house with strip on bottom.

11. Assemble the hearts, homes, and saying.

12. Add the 2" x 30½" background strips to the top and bottom of the wall hanging and the 2" x 33½" background strips to each side.

13. Sew the 1½" x 33½" red print inner border strips to the top and bottom of the quilt and the 1½" x 35½" red print inner border strips to each side.

14. Add the 3½" x 35½" dark blue outer border strips to the top and bottom of the wall hanging and the 3½" x 41½" dark blue outer border strips to each side.

15. Referring to General Instructions on pages 6-7, layer, quilt, and bind the wall hanging.

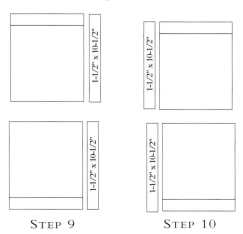

STEP 9   **STEP 10**

CUTTING

1. From gold fabric, cut one 1½" square per block (#1) for log center.
2. From 1" strips, cut ONE per block of the following lengths:

Lights	Darks
#2 – 1½"	#4 – 2"
#3 – 2"	#5 – 2½"
#6 – 2½"	#8 – 3"
#7 – 3"	#9 – 3½"
#10 – 3½"	#12 – 4"
#11 – 4"	#13 – 4½"
#14 – 4½"	#16 – 5"
#15 – 5"	#17 – 5½"
#18 – 5½"	#20 – 6"
#19 – 6"	#21 – 6½"

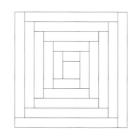

STEP 2

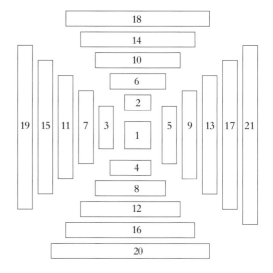

ASSEMBLY

1. Each strip is cut to size. Press away from center. Then measure block each time a strip is added. If necessary, adjust seam allowances to ensure accuracy of the block size. The completed log blocks should measure 6½" square.

2. Beginning with the 1½" gold square (#1), build the log cabin blocks. Add piece #2, press, and measure. Continue piecing the log cabin, following the illustration below.

BIAS RECTANGLE INSTRUCTIONS

Cutting

1. Measurements are given for each pattern in the Cutting and Assembly Instructions.

Marking

1. You will usually need a Right and Left Bias Rectangle. It is important to mark and sew them correctly. Always refer to the diagrams when in doubt. All pattern instructions will indicate how many, and if Right, Left, or if both Bias Rectangles are needed

   a. On the right side of the background fabric, mark ⅛" from the outside edges as shown.

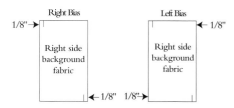

   b. On the wrong side of the contrasting fabric, mark ⅛" from the outside edges as shown.

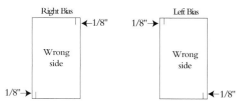

2. Notice Right and Left Bias Rectangle markings are opposite. With right sides together, the background fabric is ALWAYS on the bottom, and the contract fabric is always on the top.

   a. On the contract pieces only, (wrong side,) draw a diagonal line from⅛" upper corner marking, to ⅛" lower corner marking.

Sewing

1. With right sides together, lay the contrast piece on top of the background piece.

   a. To make the RIGHT Bias Rectangle: Turn the contrast fabric piece counter clockwise until the upper right-hand corner of the contract piece is within ⅛" of the upper left-hand corner of the back ground piece, and the lower left hand corner of the contract is within ⅛" of the lower right-hand corner of the background.

   b. To make a LEFT Bias Rectangle: Turn the contrast fabric piece clockwise so that the upper left hand corner of the contrast is with in ⅛" of the upper right hand corner of the background, and the lower right-hand corner of the contrast is within ⅛" of the lower left hand-corner of the background.

   c. Sew on the drawn line marked on contrast fabric.

   d. Cut away contrast fabric only and leave a ¼" seam allowance on either side of the sewing line. Open and press.

   e. If making more than one Bias Rectangle, chain or clothesline stitch them together.

Note: Always assemble one Bias Rectangle and check that it is correct. To help remember which way to turn the contrast. Right BR turns left, and Left BR turns right.

RIGHT BIAS RECTANGLES STEP 2 & 2A

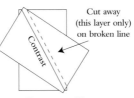

RIGHT BIAS RECTANGLES STEP 1A

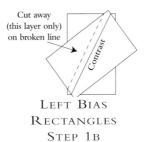

LEFT BIAS RECTANGLES STEP 1B

CUTTING

1. For the logs, cut an assortment of dark, medium dark, and light strips 1" wide. See Log Cabin Blocks, page 159.

2. From assorted fabrics, cut one 3½" x 4" rectangle and two 1¼" x 3" rectangle for house front, one 2" x 3" rectangle for door, two 2" x 2½" rectangles for roof pitch, one 2½" x 5" rectangles and two 2" x 2½" rectangles for roof, and two 1½" squares for chimneys.

3. From background fabric, cut two 2" x 2½" rectangles, two 1½" x 2" rectangles, and one 1½" x 4½" rectangles.

ASSEMBLY

1. Make Bias Rectangles

   a. Referring to page 159, make one LEFT Bias Rectangle using a 2" x 2½" background rectangle and a roof pitch 2" x 2½" rectangle.

   b. Make one RIGHT Bias Rectangle, using a 2" x 2½" roof pitch rectangle and a 2" x 2½" roof rectangle. (The roof piece will be on the bottom.)

   c. Make one RIGHT bias rectangle using a 2" x 2½" roof rectangle and a 2" x 2½" background rectangle.

2. Assemble the roof section using illustration below as a guide. This unit measures 2½" x 9½".

2-1/2" x 5-1/2"

3. Assemble the house front and add log block. Notice the placement of light and dark on the log block. This unit measures $6\frac{1}{2}$" x $9\frac{1}{2}$".

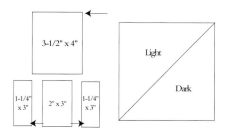

4. Assemble the chimney strip.

5. Assemble the house. House block measures $9\frac{1}{2}$" x $9\frac{1}{2}$".

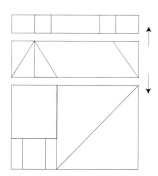

Heart Blocks

CUTTING

1. From gold, cut one $2\frac{1}{2}$" square per block. This is #1 piece in the log block.

2. From background, cut two $5\frac{1}{2}$" squares, two $2\frac{1}{2}$" squares, one $1\frac{1}{2}$" x $4\frac{1}{2}$" rectangle, and one $1\frac{1}{2}$" x $2\frac{1}{2}$" rectangle, per block.

3. From dark and medium dark, cut $1\frac{1}{2}$" x 44" strips.

4. From $1\frac{1}{2}$" strips, cut one per block of the following lengths:
   #2—$2\frac{1}{2}$", #3—$3\frac{1}{2}$", #4—$3\frac{1}{2}$", #5—$4\frac{1}{2}$", #6—$4\frac{1}{2}$", #7—$5\frac{1}{2}$",
   #8—$5\frac{1}{2}$", #9—$6\frac{1}{2}$", #10—$3\frac{1}{2}$" (cut two per block), #11—$7\frac{1}{2}$", #12—$7\frac{1}{2}$", #13—$8\frac{1}{2}$", #14—$4\frac{1}{2}$" (cut two per block), #15—$9\frac{1}{2}$", #16—$9\frac{1}{2}$", #17—$10\frac{1}{2}$".

ASSEMBLY

1. Beginning with the $2\frac{1}{2}$" gold square center (#1), build the log cabin blocks, ending with Strip 9.

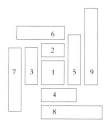

2. Make Strip 10, using the $1\frac{1}{2}$" x $3\frac{1}{2}$" pieces and the $1\frac{1}{2}$" x $2\frac{1}{2}$" background pieces. Place fabrics right sides together and draw a diagonal line on the wrong side of the fabric from corner to corner. Stitch on the diagonal line just drawn and cut away $\frac{1}{4}$" from the sewn line on the top fabric only. Open and press.

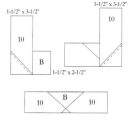

3. Continue assembling the block. Stop after adding Strip 13.

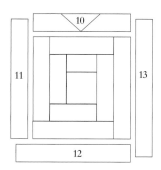

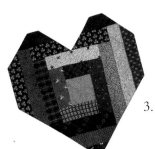

4. Make Strip 14 using the 1½" x 4½" #14 pieces and the 1½" x 4½" background piece, using same method as used in Step 2.

5. Continue assembling the block. Block measures 10½" square.

6. Draw diagonal lines on the 2½" background squares, place the squares at each top corner of the heart block, stitch, press, and trim.

7. Draw diagonal lines on the 5½" background squares, place the squares at the bottom corners of the heart block, stitch, press, and trim.

STEP 4

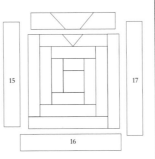

STEP 5

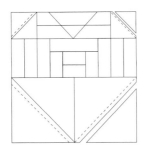

Finished size 46" x 52½"

MATERIALS

- ⅓ yard of plaid fabric for background for stars
- ⅛ yard of gold print fabric for stars
- ¼ yard tan print for background for trees
- ⅛ yard of green fabric for trees
- ⅛ yard of brown fabric for tree trunk
- ½ yard blue fabric for sashing
- ⅛ yard red check for cornerstones
- ⅛ yard of five assorted light plaids for background for houses
- ⅛ yard each of darks, medium, darks, and lights or scraps for 9 house blocks
- ⅓ yard of red fabric for inner border
- ½ yard of blue plaid for outer border

CUTTING

1. See House Blocks on page 160 for cutting instruction for houses.

2. From plaid fabric for background for stars, cut two 2¾" x 3½" rectangles, three 3½" x 5½" rectangles, four 3½" x 5⅜" rectangles, two 3½" squares, twenty-two 1½" x 2½" rectangles, and forty-four 1½" squares.

3. From gold print for stars, cut eleven 1½" x 3½" rectangles and twenty-two 1½" squares.

4. From tan print for tree background, cut two 1½" x 4" rectangles, four 4" x 4¾" rectangles, ten 2" squares, and ten 2½" squares.

5. From green fabric for trees, cut five 2½" x 4½" rectangles for trees.

6. From brown fabric for tree trunks, cut five 1½" x 2" reectangles for tree trunks.

7. From plaid fabric for house background, for each house block cut one 1½" x 9½" rectangle and two 1½" x 10½" rectangles. Four fabrics may be used twice.

8. From blue fabric, cut twelve 2" x 10½" rectangles and twelve 2" x 11½" rectangles for the sashing.

9. From red check fabric, cut sixteen 2" squares for cornerstones.

10. From red fabric, cut six 1½" x 42" strips for inner border.

11. From blue plaid fabric, cut six 3" x 42" strips for outer border.

ASSEMBLY

1. For house blocks, see page 160. Make 9 blocks. Sew one 1½" x 9½" plaid rectangle of matching plaid to the bottom of each house unit, and sew 1½" x 10½" matching plaid rectangle to each side of each house unit.

2. Sew three houses and four 2" x 10½" blue sashing rectangles together to make a row. Make three rows.

3. Sew four 2" red check squares to three 2" x 11½" blue sashing rectangles to make a horizontal sashing row. Make four.

4. To make a tree unit, position a 2½" tan print square on the corner of a 4½" green rectangle. Draw a diagonal line on the tan print square and stitch

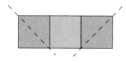

ASSEMBLY—
STEP 4

ASSEMBLY—
STEP 8

ASSEMBLY—
STEP 8

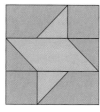

ASSEMBLY—
STEP 8B

on the line. Trim the seam allowance to ¼" and press toward the triangle. Repeat the process on the opposite corner. Make five tree top units.

5. Sew 2" tan print squares to both sides of the brown 1½" x 2" rectangles. Make five tree-trunk units.

6. Sew the tree-trunk unit to the treetop unit. Make five.

7. Connect the tree units by sewing a 4" x 4¾" rectangle between each tree unit. Now sew a 1½" x 4" rectangle to both ends of the strip.

8. To make the star units, place a 1½" plaid background square on the corners of the 1½" x 3½" gold rectangles. Draw a diagonal line corner to corner. Sew on line and trim a ¼" and press. Make eleven.

    a. Place a 1½" gold square on the corner of each 1½" x 2½" plaid rectangle. Draw a diagonal line on the gold squares and stitch on this line. Make twenty-two.

    b. Sew a 1½" plaid background square to the gold end of each rectangle. Sew these units to the top and bottom of the first unit.

9. For the bottom row of stars, starting at the left, attach in the following order: star, 3½" square, star, 3½" x 5½" rectangle, star, 3½" x 5½" rectangle, star, 3½" x 5½" rectangle, star, 3½" square, star.

10. For the top row of stars, starting at the left, attach in the following order: 2¾" x 3½" rectangle, star, 3½" x 5⅜" rectangle, star, 3½" x 5⅜", rectangle, star, 3½" x 5⅜" rectangle, star, 3½" x 5⅜" rectangle, star, 2¾" x 3½" rectangle.

11. Cut two 1½" x 39½" (measure your quilt for your exact measurement) inner border strips from the red fabric

and attach to the top and bottom of the quilt. Press toward the border.

12. Diagonally piece three 1½" x 42" red strips and cut two pieces 48" (or your exact measurement). Attach to the sides of the quilt. Press toward the border.

13. Cut two strips of blue plaid border fabric 41½". Be sure to check your quilt for the exact measurement.

14. Sew two 41½" green plaid strips to the top and bottom of the quilt. Press toward the border.

15. Diagonally piece two 3" x 42" green plaid strips to make the side border strip and cut 53½" (or your exact measurement) and attach to one side. Press toward the border. Repeat for the opposite side.

16. Refer to General Instructions on page 7 for finishing the quilt.

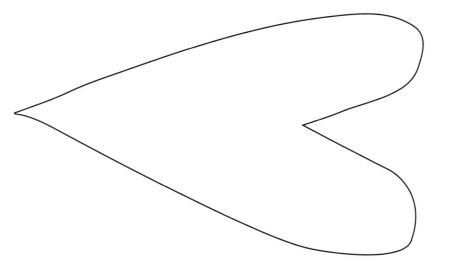

Refer to General Instructions on page 7 for finishing the quilt.

Framed Heart 'n Home Picture

MATERIALS

- 7½" x 14" purchased frame
- ⅓ yard of light tan fabric for background
- ⅓ yard flannel
- ⅓ yard needlepunch
- Assorted dark, medium, and light fabric scraps
- Black and red embroidery floss

CUTTING

1. Cut dimensions shown in the log cabin illustration shown on page 159 for strips #1 through #13 only for the log cabin square.

2. From background fabric, cut two 3" x 4½" rectangles and one 3½" x 10½" rectangle.

3. From background fabric, cut one 9½" x 10½" rectangle.

ASSEMBLY

1. Assemble the log cabin block, piecing Strips #1 through #13 only.

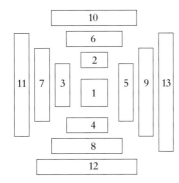

2. Add the background strips to the top, bottom, left side, and then right side as shown in the illustration.

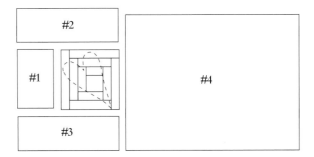

3. Trace the words onto the background fabric, below. To determine word placement, place the frame over the panel. Lightly draw a pencil line around the area to be embroidered. Cut a piece of flannel to fit the whole panel and iron to the background piece. Embroider words and hearts.

4. Quilt a large heart through the log cabin block. Use heart pattern on page 164.

5. Measure the inside of the frame, and cut two pieces of cardboard and one piece of needlepunch this size. Glue the needlepunch to one piece of cardboard.

6. Center and lay the picture right side up on the needlepunch. Trim the edges of the fabric so they are one inch larger than the cardboard piece.

7. Bring the edges of the fabric to the back side of the cardboard and glue.

8. Place the picture in the frame, put glue around the edges of the back of the picture, and lay the remaining piece of cardboard on top to hide the raw edges of the picture.

Where memories are made
And quilts are sewn
This is a place
Called heart and home

♡ ♡ ♡ ♡ ♡ ♡

Where friendships are formed
And families are grown
Where joy is shared
And true love is known
Where memories are made
And quilts are sewn
This is a place
Called heart and home ♡

♡ ♡ ♡ ♡ ♡ ♡

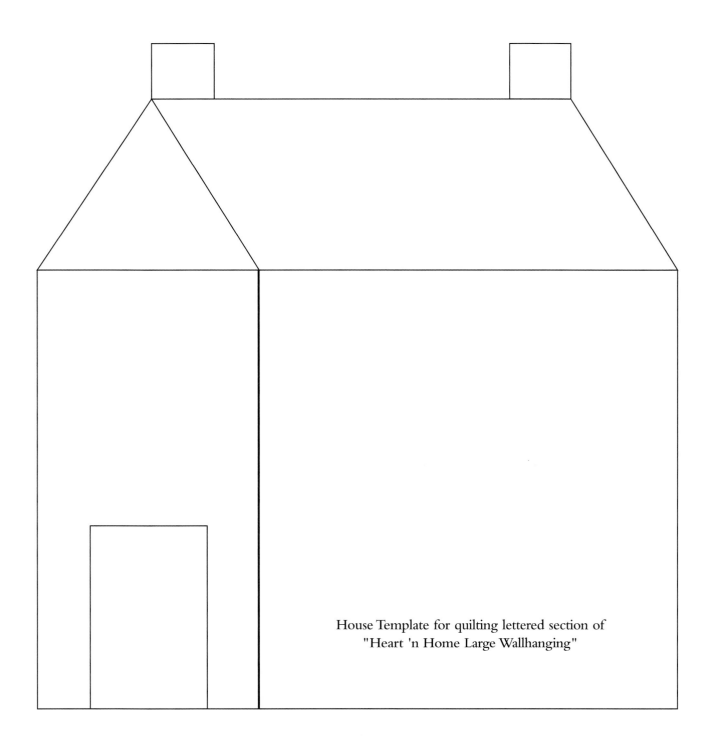

House Template for quilting lettered section of
"Heart 'n Home Large Wallhanging"

Jill Reber

INDIAN SUMMER

Jill Reber has been sewing for as long as she can remember and quilting for more than twenty years. It was a natural progression from sewing doll clothes to her own clothing to quilting. That led to teaching, designing, and a line of patterns. To make measuring and cutting easier for quilters, Jill, along with husband Jim developed a line of Master Piece Products (515/999-2746) allowing the quilter to cut multiple pieces of fabric quickly and safely. Jill has completed more than 100 quilts using the Master Piece Method.

In addition to running a small company, Jill is active in the Des Moines Area Quilt Guild with an impressive membership of more than 500 quilters serving as Quilt Show chair in 1999 and in 2004. Much of Jill's time is now spent designing patterns and projects for publications. Designing with traditional quilt blocks is her favorite style of quilting. For the year 2000 Jill was selected to design six quilts and the annual sampler quilt for Better Homes and Gardens® *American Patchwork & Quilting*.

In addition to designing for publications, Jill is also a talented technical editor and stylist for photography. Many of her projects such as the Indian Summer wallhanging are designed with seasonal home decorating in mind.

MATERIALS

- Eight 2½" x 12" green rectangles for trees.
- ¼ yard of brown fabric for tree trunk.
- 1½" yards of dark green fabric for borders.
- ¼ yard solid tan background for center tree block
- 1 fat quarter tan check fabric for corner triangles
- Assorted tan print fabrics to equal approximately ¾ yard
- Assorted scraps of brown plaid, green check, peach, rusts, golds, and browns
- 2¾ yard for backing
- 49" x 51" piece of batting

Indian Summer Wallhanging

Finished size 45" x 47"

CUTTING

1. From six assorted brown fabrics, cut six 5¼" squares for flying geese units. Cut these squares diagonally twice for twenty-four triangles.

2. From six assorted tan background fabrics for flying geese units, cut twenty-four 2⅞" squares. Cut these squares in half diagonally for forty-eight triangles.

3. Refer to House Block on page 177 templates. Cut two houses from assorted rust, brown, and tan fabrics. Reverse the cutting of Template D for two of the houses so that the houses face toward the center of the quilt.

4. For dark side of house, from gold fabric, cut, four 1½" x 3½" rectangles, and four 1½" x 5½" rectangles, from rust fabric, cut four 1½" x 3½" rectangles, and four 1½" x 5½" rectangles, and from beige/tan fabrics, cut twenty-four 1½" squares.

169

5. For light side of house, from peach fabric, cut four 2½" x 3½" rectangles, and two 2½" x 4½" rectangles, from gold fabric, cut four 2½" x 3½" rectangles, and two 2½" x 4½" rectangles, and from brown fabric, cut four 2½" x 3½" rectangles.
6. For chimney unit, from rust fabric cut, eight 1¼" x 2¼" squares, and from assorted tan prints, cut eight 1¼" x 2¾" rectangles, and four 1¼" x 3¼" rectangles.
7. From the eight assorted green fabrics, cut 2½" x 12" rectangles for trees. Cut eight of templates A, B, and C for Little Pine Blocks.

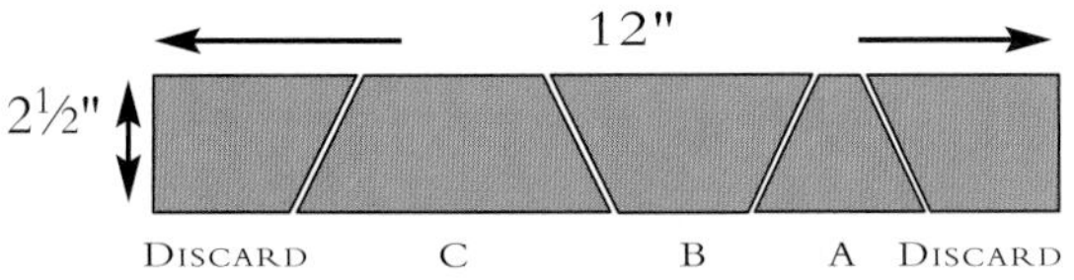
12"
2½"
DISCARD
C
B
A
DISCARD

8. From assorted tan background fabrics, cut eight 2½" x 12" strips for tree units. Using templates 1L, 1R, 2L, 2R, 3L, and 3R on page 178 or a ruler with a 60° angle, cut eight of templates 1L, 1R, 2L, 2R, 3L, and 3R.

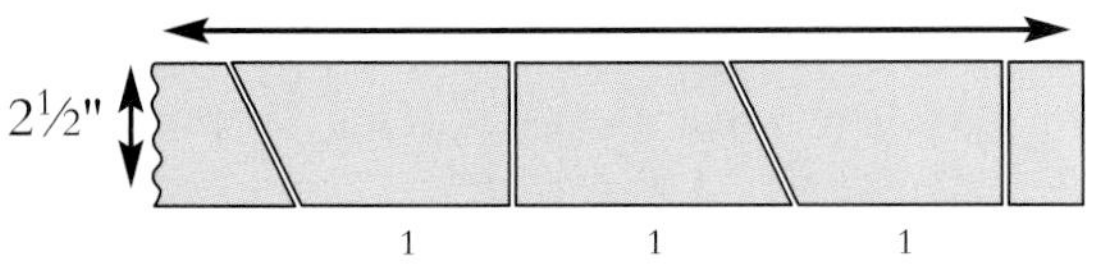
2½"
1
1
1

9. From brown print fabric, cut eight 1½" squares for tree trunks.
10. From assorted tan background fabrics, cut 1½" x 3" rectangles for trunk units. Cut eight 1½" x 6½" rectangles and six 2½" x 2½" squares to be sewn to tree units.
11. From brown plaid fabric, cut eight 2⅞" squares for Indian Summer Blocks. Cut squares in half diagonally for sixteen triangles.

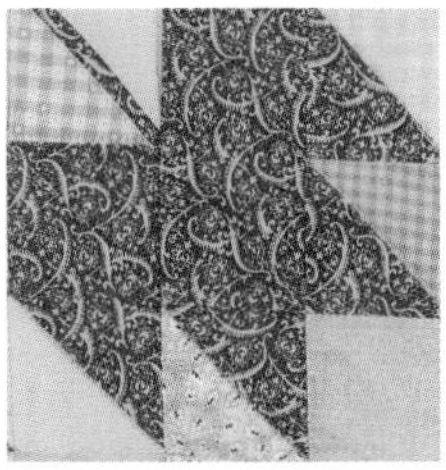

MAPLE-LEAF BLOCK STEP 15

CENTER TREE BLOCK STEP 17

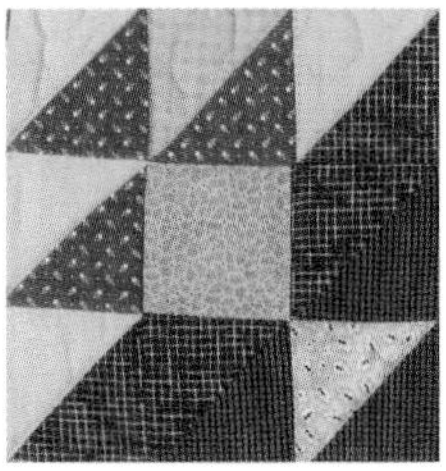

INDIAN SUMMER BLOCK STEP 11

12. From green check fabric, cut six 2⅞" squares for 9-patch blocks. Cut squares in half diagonally for twelve triangles.
13. From peach print fabric, cut six 2⅞" squares for 9-patch blocks. Cut squares in half diagonally for twelve triangles.
14. From assorted tan background prints, cut twelve 2⅞" squares and four 2½" squares for 9-patch blocks. Cut the 2⅞" squares in half diagonally for twenty-four triangles.
15. From each of four assorted print fabrics, cut three 2½" squares, two 2⅞" squares, and one ⅞" x 5" rectangle for the maple-leaf block. Cut the 2⅞" squares in half diagonally for four triangles.
16. From assorted tan background prints, cut four 2½" squares, eight 2⅞" squares for the maple-leaf backgrounds, and four 2⅝" squares for the stem-square background. Cut the 2⅝" squares in half diagonally for sixteen triangles.
17. From assorted rust fabrics, cut twenty 2⅜" squares for the center tree. Cut the squares in half diagonally to make forty triangles.
18. From solid tan background fabric, cut four 2" squares, Template D, left and rights, one 3⅝" square, and sixteen 2⅜" squares for the center tree. Cut the 2⅜"squares in half diagonally to make thirty-two triangles, and cut the 3⅝" square in half diagonally to make two triangles.
19. From brown fabric for the tree trunk, cut one 5⅛" square. Cut in half diagonally to make two triangles. Cut one 2½" x 5¾" triangle and one 1⅞" square, cut in half diagonally.
20. From dark green border fabric, cut four 1¾" x 14" rectangles,

two 1½" x 24½" rectangles, two 1½" x 22½" rectangles, two 1½" x 43" strips, three 2½" x 43" strips for borders, and five 2¼" x 43" strips for binding.

21. From gold fabric, cut four 1¾" squares for cornerstones.

22. From tan check, cut two 11⅞" squares. Cut in half diagonally to make four triangles for corners of center block.

23. From assorted tan print fabrics, cut twenty-four 1½" x 7½" or 8½" rectangles for tree borders.

ASSEMBLY

1. To make the flying geese units, sew the assorted tan background fabric triangles to the right side of the twenty-four brown fabric triangles. Sew the remaining assorted tan background triangles to the left side of the units. Units should measure 2½" x 4½". Sew twelve flying geese units together. Make two.

2. To make house blocks, sew the dark side of house, light side of house, roof units and chimney units together. Make four house blocks.

3. Following the diagram below, sew eight tree blocks.

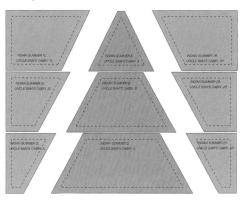

HOUSE
BLOCK
STEP 2

4. Sew tan background fabric 1½" x 3" rectangles to both sides of the brown fabric 1½" squares for tree trunks. Make four. Sew to the bottom of four tree units. Sew a tan background fabric 1½" x 6½" rectangle to the top of two of these units and to the bottom of two of these units for a total of eight Little Pine Blocks.

5. Sew three tan background fabric 2½" squares together. Make two. Press and sew to the top of one tree unit and to the bottom of one tree unit.

6. Sew a tan background fabric 1½" x 6½" rectangle to the top and bottom of the remaining two tree units.

7. For Indian Summer blocks sew eight green triangles to eight brown plaid triangles, sew four green triangles to four tan background triangles, sew twelve peach triangles to twelve tan background triangles, and sew eight brown plaid triangles to eight tan background triangles. Sew the squares and the rows together. Make four 9-patch blocks.

9. To make the maple-leaf blocks, sew the assorted print fabric 2⅞" half-square triangles to the background fabric 2⅞" half-square triangles. Sew the background 2⅝" half-square triangles to the stem fabric ⅞" x 5" rectangles. Assemble the blocks.

STEM

CLIP

10. To make center block, sew together thirty-two assorted rust fabric $2\frac{3}{8}$" half-square triangles and thirty-two tan background fabric $2\frac{3}{8}$" half-square triangles.

11. To make the tree-trunk unit, sew the $1\frac{7}{8}$" half-square triangle at the x side of Template D. Sew these units to the sides of the brown tree-trunk fabric $2\frac{1}{2}$" x $5\frac{3}{4}$" rectangle. Center and sew the brown tree-trunk fabric $5\frac{1}{8}$" half-square triangle to the top of the unit just sewn.

12. Sew the tan background fabric $3\frac{5}{8}$" half-square triangle to the bottom of the tree trunk. Trim the block as needed and sew to the small tree unit. Sew the two pieces together.

13. Sew two dark green fabric $1\frac{3}{4}$" x 14" rectangles to the sides of the center tree block. Sew gold fabric $1\frac{3}{4}$" squares to the ends of the remaining two dark green fabric $1\frac{3}{4}$" x 14" rectangles and sew to the remaining two sides.

14. Sew the tan check fabric triangles to the four sides of the square. Press toward the triangles.

15. Sew the dark green fabric $1\frac{1}{2}$" x $22\frac{1}{2}$" rectangles to the sides of the center square. Press. Sew the dark green fabric $1\frac{1}{2}$" x $24\frac{1}{2}$" rectangles to the top and bottom of the square.

16. Assemble the two side units and attach to the sides of the center block.

17. Randomly sew together the $1\frac{1}{2}$" x $7\frac{1}{2}$" or $8\frac{1}{2}$" assorted tan print fabric rectangles. Cut one strip $24\frac{1}{2}$" long and sew to the top of the top-row tree unit. Sew a house square to each end of the tree unit. From the tan print strip, cut a strip $41\frac{1}{2}$" long and sew to the bottom of the top row just assembled.

MAKE 1
STEP 10.

MAKE 1
STEP 10.

MAKE 1
STEP 10.

From the tan print, cut two 10 strips and sew to both sides of the top row. Attach the top row to the center of the quilt.

18. Following the same cutting and sewing instructions from Step 17, make the bottom row and attach to the bottom of the quilt.

19. Measure the length of the quilt, and cut the $1\frac{1}{2}$" dark green border strips to that measurement. Sew the border strips to the sides of the quilt. Press toward the border.

20. Piece the $2\frac{1}{2}$" dark green border strips. Measure the width of the quilt, and cut two strips to that measurement. Sew the border strips to the top and bottom of the quilt. Press toward the border.

21. Refer to General Instructions on page 6 for instructions for finishing the quilt.

Finished size 24" square

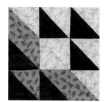

ASSEMBLY—
STEP 1

ASSEMBLY—
STEP 2

MATERIALS

- ¼ yard tan print fabric for background
- ¼ yard of gold, rust, plum, and dark green or scraps of these colors
- ¼ yard brown leaf fabric for border
- ¼ yard dark green print for binding
- ⅞ yard of fabric for backing
- 28" square of batting

CUTTING

1. From the tan print background fabric, cut eight 3½" squares. Cut ten 3⅞" squares and cut them in half diagonally for twenty triangles.

2. From the dark green, cut six 3⅞" squares. Cut the squares in half diagonally to make twelve triangles.

3. From plum fabric, cut six 3⅞" squares. Cut the squares in half diagonally to make twelve triangles.

4. From gold fabric, cut five 3⅞" squares. Cut the squares in half diagonally to make ten triangles.

5. From the rust fabric, cut five 3⅞" squares. Cut the squares in half diagonally to make ten triangles.

6. From brown leaf fabric, cut four 3½" x 18½" rectangles for border.

7. From dark green print, cut three 2½" x 42" strips for binding.

ASSEMBLY

1. Sew together tan print background fabric 3⅞" half-square triangles with six dark green fabric half-square triangles, six plum fabric half-square triangles, four gold fabric half-square triangles, and four rust fabric half-square triangles.

2. Sew together six gold fabric and six dark green fabric half-square triangles.

3. Sew together six plum fabric and six rust fabric half-square triangles.

4. Following the diagram, sew the blocks together for each row, and then sew the rows together.

5. Sew 3½" x 18½" rectangles to the sides of the quilt.

6. Sew 3½" tan print background fabric squares to both ends of the remaining two 3½" x 18½" rectangles. Then sew these border strips to the top and bottom of the quilt.

7. Refer to General Instructions on page 6 for instructions for finishing the quilt.

Uncle Sam's Cabin

Finished size 20" x 30"

MATERIALS

- ½ neutral fabric for background
- ½ yard navy plaid fabric for inner border and binding
- ½ yard tan plaid fabric for outer border
- Assorted scraps of green, blue, red, natural, and brown for blocks
- ⅔ yard of fabric for backing
- 24" x 34" piece of batting

CUTTING

1. From neutral background fabric, cut two 1¼" x 2¾" rectangles, one 1¼" x 3½" rectangle, and one 1¼" x 9½" rectangle for the chimney unit. Cut two 1½" x 9½" rectangles and one 1½" x 11½" rectangle for the house block. Cut two Template F (page 179), left and right rectangles for the roof unit. Cut four Template F (page 179), left and right rectangles and two 1¼" x 4½" rectangles for tree-trunk background. Cut two 1½" x 7½" rectangles and two 1½" x 4½" rectangles for flag blocks.

2. From the navy plaid fabric, cut two 1½" x 42" strips for the inner border, three 2¼" x 42" strips for the binding, and a Template D strip for the roof.

3. From tan plaid fabric, cut three 4" x 42" strips for outer border.

4. Cutting from assorted scraps of fabric will be given with instructions for assembly of each block.

ASSEMBLY

House Blocks

1. Cut two 1¼" squares from red fabric for chimneys.

2. Sew a 1¼" chimney square to each end of the neutral background fabric 1¼" x 3½" rectangle. Then sew background fabric 1¼" x 2¾" rectangles to both ends.

3. Sew the neutral background fabric 1¼" x 9½" rectangle to the top of the chimney unit.

4. Cut one light blue check Template E, on page 178.

5. From light background fabric, cut one Template F, left and right, on page 178.

6. From navy plaid, cut 1 Template D, for the roof (page 178).

7. For the roof unit, sew D to E. Add F triangles to both sides.

8. Sew chimney unit to roof unit. Press.

9. For the light side of house, cut two 1½" x 3½" rectangles and one 1½" x 4½" rectangle from red fabric. Cut one 2½" x 3½" rectangle for door from red stripe fabric. Sew the pieces together to make the unit.

10. For the dark side of the house, cut three 1½" squares from one light fabric and three 1½" squares from a different light fabric for windows. Cut two 1½" x 2½" rectangles and two 1½" x 5½" rectangles from dark red fabric. Sew the pieces together to make the unit.

11. Sew the light side of the house to the dark side of the house.

12. Sew the house unit to the roof unit. Press. Sew the 1½" x 9½" rectangles of background fabric to the sides of the cabin. Sew the 1½" x 11½" rectangle to the bottom of the cabin. Press.

Tree Blocks

1. From dark green fabric, cut two Template E, cut two Template F, right, and two Template L, right (page 179).

2. From neutral fabric, cut two template F, Right (page 179) and two Template F, Left.

3. Sew the neutral fabric triangles to the sides of the tree triangles, as shown.

4. From brown fabric, cut two 1" x 1¼" rectangles for tree trunks. Sew the neutral background fabric 1¼" x 2¼" rectangles to both sides of the tree trunks. Sew the neutral background fabric 1¼" x 4½" rectangles to the bottom of each unit.

5. Sew the trunk units to the tree units.

Flag Blocks

1. Cut two 2½" x 3½" rectangles from navy star fabric, four 1½" x 7½"

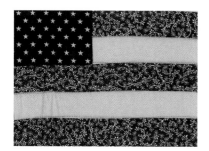

rectangles and two 1½" x 4½" rectangles from red fabric. Sew one 1½" x 4½" background fabric rectangle to one 1½" x 4½" red fabric rectangle. Repeat for second flag. Sew 2½" x 3½" navy star fabric rectangles to the left of the stripe units.

2. For each flag, sew a 1½" x 7½" red fabric rectangle to the top and bottom of a 1½"" x 7½" background fabric rectangle.

3. Sew the two units together. Press.

ASSEMBLY OF QUILT

1. Following the layout in the picture, shown shown on page 176, sew the flag and tree units together. Press seam towards the flag. Sew these rows to the top and bottom of the cabin. Press.

2. Measure the length of the quilt and cut two strips this measurement from the navy plaid fabric 1½" strips for the inner border. Sew the strips to both sides of the quilt. Press toward the border.

3. Measure the width of the quilt, including the border strips just attached, and cut two strips this measurement from the navy plaid fabric 1½" strips. Sew the strips to the top and bottom of the quilt. Press toward the border.

4. Measure the width of the quilt and cut two strips this measurement from the tan plaid fabric 4" strip for the outer border. Sew these border strips to the top and bottom of the quilt.

5. Measure the length of the quilt and cut two strips this measurement from the tan plaid fabric 4" strips for the outer border. Sew these border strips to the sides of the quilt.

6. Refer to General Instructions on page 6 for instructions for finishing the quilt.

Finished size: 18" x 18" and 4" x 4"

MATERIALS

- Four 2½ x 20" strips of assorted green fabrics for trees

- ¼ yard of dark green fabric for setting triangles and square

- ⅔ yard of off-white fabric for background and backing

- 20" square of batting for mat and four 5″ squares of batting for coasters

CUTTING

1. From dark green fabric, cut one 6½" square and one 7¼" square. Cut the 7¼" square in half diagonally twice for four triangles.

2. Using the templates A, B, and C on page 178, cut the four 2½" x 20" strips of assorted green fabrics for trees. Cut eight of templates A and B and cut four of template C.

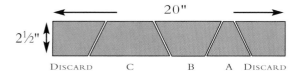

3. From the off-white background fabric, cut two 2½" x 42" strips. Using templates 1L, 1R, 2L, 2R, 3L, and 3R on page 179, cut eight of templates 1L, 1R, 2L, and 2R. Cut four of templates 3L and 3R.

ASSEMBLY

1. Following the diagram on page 171, sew four tree blocks.

2. Following the diagram below, sew the mat together.

3. Layer right sides together with batting and backing. Sew using a ¼" seam allowance, leaving an opening for turning. Turn and press. Slipstitch opening closed. Quilt as desired.

4. To make coasters, sew the top two rows of the tree together as shown in diagram on page 171. Trim the tree units to 4½" inches square.

5. Layer right sides together with batting and backing. Finish the coasters following Step 3 above.

INDIAN SUMMER 1R
UNCLE SAM'S CABIN 1R

INDIAN SUMMER 2R
UNCLE SAM'S CABIN 2R

INDIAN SUMMER 2R
UNCLE SAM'S CABIN 2R

INDIAN SUMMER A
UNCLE SAM'S CABIN A

INDIAN SUMMER B
UNCLE SAM'S CABIN B

INDIAN SUMMER C
UNCLE SAM'S CABIN C

INDIAN SUMMER 1L
UNCLE SAM'S CABIN 1L

INDIAN SUMMER 2L
UNCLE SAM'S CABIN 2L

INDIAN SUMMER 2L
UNCLE SAM'S CABIN 2L

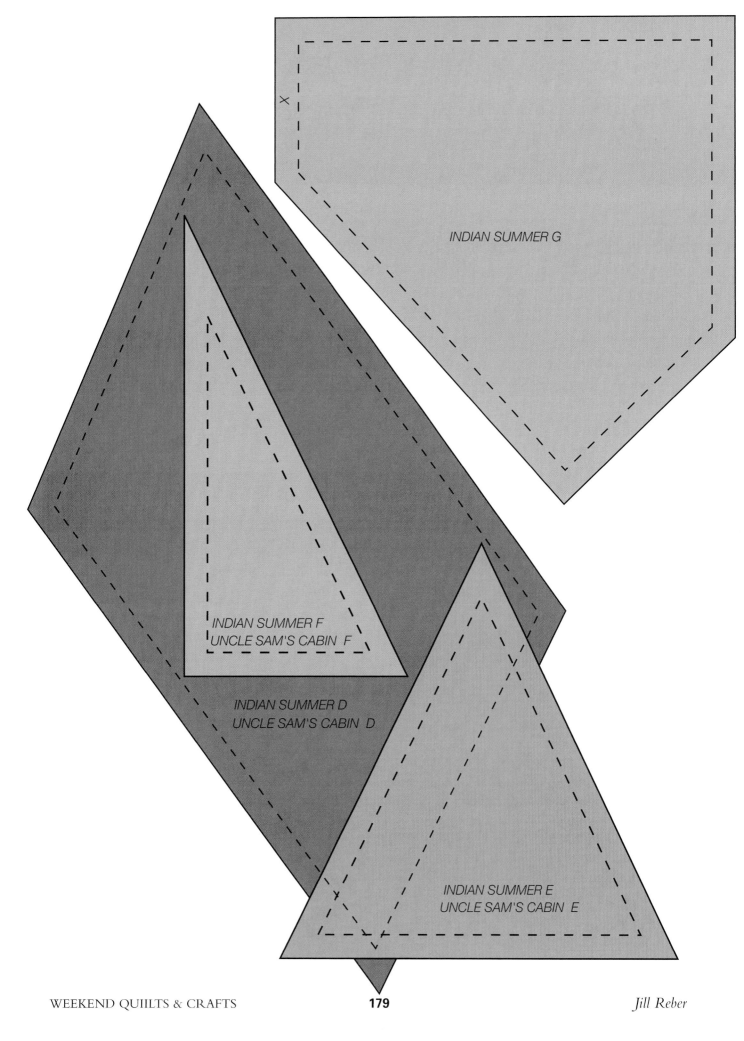

INDIAN SUMMER G

INDIAN SUMMER F
UNCLE SAM'S CABIN F

INDIAN SUMMER D
UNCLE SAM'S CABIN D

INDIAN SUMMER E
UNCLE SAM'S CABIN E

Fons & Porter

PORCH PURSUITS

When Marianne Fons and Liz Porter met in a beginners' quilting class in 1976, they were interested in a hobby that would teach them how to make beautiful quilts for their homes. Soon, Marianne and Liz were teaching classes themselves in Winterset, Iowa, in Madison County, home of the famous covered bridges.

With degrees in English, Fons & Porter added writing quilting books to their skills. In 1993, their *Quilter's Complete Guide* became one of the best selling, most widely used quilting manuals ever published. In addition, there are 15 titles currently available.

Fons & Porter's first 13-part series for Public Television began airing nationwide in 1995, and they have subsequently produced ten 13-episode series to date. In 1996, Fons & Porter's publisher, Oxmoor House, launched a bi-monthly magazine with Marianne and Liz as executive editors. In 2001, Marianne and Liz had the opportunity to purchase the magazine. Under their ownership, *Fons & Porter's Love of Quilting* now holds second place nationwide in terms of circulation.

A recent addition is a retail store in Winterset, Iowa, on the charming town square. Living in an historic town, Liz and Marianne have discovered the joys of collecting antique quilts. The Porch Pursuits collection began with a quilt top Liz discovered, had quilted, and named Antique Sherbet. The color palette was adapted for pillows and picnic accessories.

MATERIALS

- 2½ yards blue solid for blocks and binding
- 2 yards green solid for blocks
- 2 yards raspberry solid for blocks
- 2 yards orange solid for blocks
- 4¾ yards backing fabric
- Twin-size batting

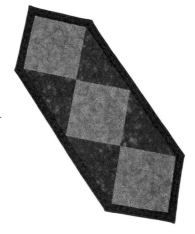

Antique Sherbet Quilt

CUTTING

Finished Size: 68" x 76½"

Blocks: 63 (8½")
Sherbet blocks

Measurements include ¼" seam allowances.

1. From blue fabric, cut 5 (3"-wide) strips. Cut strips into 64 (3") squares. Cut squares in half diagonally to make 128 A triangles. 4 (4½"-wide) strips. Cut strips into 32 (4½") C squares for block centers. 8 (1½"-wide) strips. Cut strips into 64 (1½" x 4½") D rectangles. 11 (1½"-wide) strips. Cut strips into 64 (1½" x 6½") E rectangles. 8 (2¼"-wide) strips for binding.

2. From green fabric, cut: 5 (3"-wide) strips. Cut strips into 62 (3") squares. Cut squares in half diagonally to make 124 A triangles. 4 (4½"-wide) strips. Cut strips into 31 (4½") C squares for block centers. 8 (1½"-wide) strips. Cut strips into 62 (1½" x 4½") D rectangles. 11 (1½"-wide) strips. Cut strips into 62 (1½" x 6½") E rectangles.

3. From raspberry fabric, cut: 15 (3"-wide) strips. Cut strips into 192 (3") squares. Cut the squares in half diagonally to make 384 A triangles. 8 (2½"-wide) strips. Cut strips into 128 (2½") B squares.

4. From orange fabric, cut: 15 (3"-wide) strips. Cut strips into 186 (3") squares.

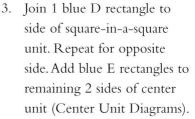

CORNER UNIT ASSEMBLY DIAGRAMS

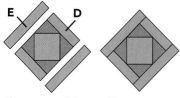

SQUARE-IN-A-SQUARE DIAGRAMS

Cut the squares in half diagonally to make 372 A triangles. 8 (2½"-wide) strips. Cut strips into 124 (2½") B squares.

BLOCK ASSEMBLY

1. Lay out 1 blue and 3 raspberry A triangles as shown in Corner Unit Assembly Diagrams. Join 1 blue triangle and 1 raspberry triangle to make a square. Join raspberry triangles to blue sides of square to complete corner unit. Make 4 corner units.

2. Referring to Square-in-a-Square Diagrams, place 1 raspberry B square atop each of 2 opposite corners of 1 blue C square, with right sides facing. Stitch diagonally as shown. Trim seams and open out to reveal triangles. Repeat on 2 remaining corners to complete square-in-a-square unit.

3. Join 1 blue D rectangle to side of square-in-a-square unit. Repeat for opposite side. Add blue E rectangles to remaining 2 sides of center unit (Center Unit Diagrams).

4. Join 1 raspberry/blue corner unit to each side of center unit. Press seam allowances toward corner units

CENTER UNIT DIAGRAMS

BLOCK ASSEMBLY DIAGRAM

(Block Assembly Diagram). Make 32 raspberry/blue Sherbet blocks (Raspberry/Blue Block Diagram).

RASPBERRY/BLUE BLOCK DIAGRAM

5. Using orange and green pieces, repeat steps 1–4 to make 31 orange/green Sherbet blocks (Orange/Green Block Diagram).

ORANGE/GREEN BLOCK DIAGRAM

QUILT ASSEMBLY

1. Lay out blocks in 9 horizontal rows with 7 blocks in each row, alternating colors as shown in Quilt Top Assembly Diagram.

2. Join blocks into rows; join rows to complete quilt top.

QUILTING AND FINISHING

1. Divide backing fabric into 2 (2⅜-yard) pieces. Cut 1 panel in half lengthwise. Sew narrow panels to sides of wide panel. Press seam allowances toward narrow panels.

2. Layer backing, batting, and quilt top; baste. Quilt as desired. Quilt shown was quilted in an overall free-motion design with variegated thread.

3. Join 2¼"-wide strips into 1 continuous piece for straight-grain French-fold binding. Add to quilt.

QUILT TOP ASSEMBLY DIAGRAM

Finished size 17" square

MATERIALS

- ¼ yard raspberry batik (orange) for the block
- ⅝ yard bright dark blue swirl fabric (turquoise) for the block, pillow back, and cording.
- 2 yards ⅜" cording
- 16" pillow form
- If making the turquoise and orange pillow, substitute orange for raspberry and turquoise for dark blue.

CUTTING

1. From the raspberry batik fabric, cut one 8½" square(C), two 2½" x 8½" rectangles(D), and two 2½" x 12½" rectangles(E), two 4⅞" squares(A). Cut the 4⅞" squares in half diagonally.

2. From the dark blue swirl fabric, cut two 1½" x 42" strips for the cording, one 17" square for the pillow back, and four 4⅞" squares(B), and six 4⅞" squares(A). Cut the 4⅞" squares in half diagonally for twelve triangles.

ASSEMBLY

1. Lay out one raspberry batik and three blue swirl fabric A triangles as shown in Corner Unit Assembly Diagrams. Join one blue swirl fabric triangle and one raspberry batik triangle to make a

CORNER UNIT ASSEMBLY
DIAGRAMS

square. Join blue swirl fabric triangle to raspberry batik triangle sides of the square to complete corner unit. Make four corner units.

2. Referring to Square-in-a-Square Diagrams, place one blue swirl fabric"B square atop each of two opposite corners of the raspberry batik C square, with right sides facing. Stitch diagonally as shown. Trim seams and press toward triangles. Repeat on the two remaining corners.

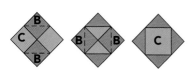

SQUARE-IN-A-SQUARE DIAGRAMS

3. Join raspberry batik D rectangles to opposite corners of square-in-a-square unit. Press toward rectangles. Sew raspberry batik E rectangles to remaining two sides.

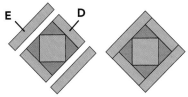

CENTER UNIT DIAGRAMS

4. Join one raspberry/blue unit to each side of center unit. See Center Unit Diagram.
5. Diagonally piece the 1¾" strips that have been cut for the cording. Lay the cord for the piping in the center of the wrong side of the strip. Fold and pin the fabric over the cord, with the raw edges even. Using a zipper foot, sew close to the cord along the length of the strip. Trim so there is a ¼" seam allowance.
6. Attach the piping to the block by aligning the raw cut edge of the piping with the raw edge of the right side of the pillow top. Using a basting stitch and the zipper foot, baste the piping in place.
7. Place the pillow front and back right sides together, and pin the layers together. Using the basted seam line as a guide, sew through both fabric layers, leaving an opening along one of the sides. Trim the corners and turn the pillow right side out. Insert the pillow form, and stitch the opening closed using a slipstitch and also slipstitch diagonally where the piping comes together.

Finished size 25" x 33"

MATERIALS

- ¾ yard of raspberry batik for blocks
- ¼ yard of dark blue fabric for blocks
- ¾ yard of turquoise fabric for sashing and border
- ⅝ yard of orange print fabric for binding
- 29" x 37" fabric for backing
- 29" x 37" piece of batting

CUTTING

1. From the raspberry batik fabric, cut twelve 4¾" (C) squares and twenty-four 3⅞" squares. Cut the squares in half diagonally for forty-eight (A) triangles.
2. From the dark blue fabric, cut forty-eight 2⅝" (B) squares.
3. From the turquoise fabric, cut nine 2" x 6½" rectangles, two 2" x 42" strips, and four 3" x 42" strips for the sashing and border.
4. From the orange print, cut strips 4½" wide for the binding.

ASSEMBLY

1. Draw a diagonal line from corner to opposite corner on the dark blue (B) squares. Place a square on the corner of a raspberry batik 4¾" (C) square and stitch on the drawn line. Press toward the corner and trim to a ¼" seam allowance. Repeat on the remaining corners of each square.

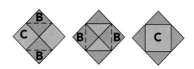

SQUARE-IN-A-SQUARE DIAGRAMS

2. Sew the raspberry batik (A) triangles to opposite corners of each Square-in-a-Square unit. Press toward the triangles. Repeat on the opposite corners. Press.

3. Connect four blocks by sewing 2" x 6¾" turquoise sashing rectangles to the blocks. Repeat for two more rows.

4. Connect these rows by sewing two 2" x 29" (or your measurement, if different) turquoise strips of sashing to the rows.

5. Sew the 3" x 29" (or your measurement, if different) border strips to the sides of the quilt.

6. Sew the 3" x 26" (or your measurement, if different) turquoise border strips to the top and bottom of the quilt.

7. Refer to General Instructions on page 7 for layering the basket cloth.

8. This quilt may be quilted, tacked, or tied.

Finished size 14" x 38"

MATERIALS

- ¼ yard of turquoise for blocks
- ⅜ yard of orange print for blocks
- ½ yard or one fat quarter of raspberry batik for setting triangles.
- ¼ yard blue print for border and binding
- ½ half yard of fabric for backing
- 18" x 42" piece of batting

CUTTING

1. From turquoise fabric, cut three 4½" C squares, six 1½" x 4½" rectangles for D sashing, six 1½" x 6½" rectangles for E sashing, and six 3" squares cut in half diagonally for twelve A triangles.

2. From orange print fabric, cut twelve 2½" B squares, eighteen— 3" squares cut in half diagonally for thirty-six A triangles.

3. From the raspberry batik, cut one 13" square. Cut the square diagonally twice for four setting triangles.

4. From the blue print fabric, cut three 1½" x 42" strips for the border and three 2¼" strips for the binding.

ASSEMBLY

1. Lay out one turquoise fabric and three orange print fabric A triangles as shown in Corner Unit Assembly

Diagrams. Join one turquoise fabric triangle and one orange print fabric triangle to make a square. Join orange print fabric triangles to turquoise fabric sides of the square to complete corner unit. Make twelve units.

CORNER UNIT ASSEMBLY
DIAGRAMS

2. Referring to Square-in-a-Square Diagrams, place one orange print fabric B square atop each of two opposite corners of one turquoise fabric C square, with right sides facing. Draw a line from corner to corner, and stitch on the drawn line. Trim seams and press toward the triangles. Repeat on two remaining corners to complete square-in-a-square unit. Make three.

SQUARE-IN-A-SQUARE DIAGRAMS

3. Join one turquoise fabric D rectangle to side of square-in-a-square unit. Repeat for opposite side. Add turquoise fabric E rectangles to remaining two sides of center unit. See Center Unit Diagrams.

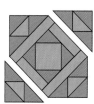

BLOCK ASSEMBLY DIAGRAM

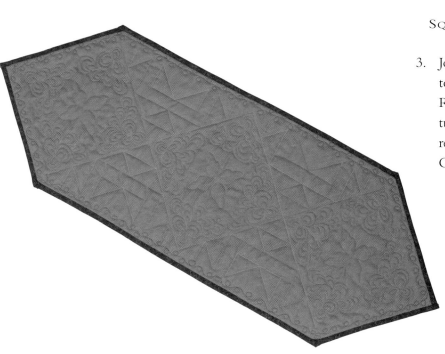

4. Join one turquoise/orange unit to each side of center unit. Press seam allowances toward corner units. See Block Assembly Diagram. Make three.

5. Assemble the blocks and setting triangles in three rows. Sew a setting triangle to the right of the block in the top row, on both sides of the block in the center row and to the left of the block in the bottom row. See Quilt Assembly Diagram. Then sew the three rows together.

6. Cut four border strips the length of the point portion of the table runner, leaving extra fabric to miter the points. Attach these four pieces of the border first, mitering both points.

7. Cut and attach two border strips for the sides of the table runner. Press and trim any excess fabric at the beginning and the end.

8. Refer to General Instructions on page 7 to layer and quilt the table runner and prepare the binding. Sew the binding to the table topper with a $\frac{1}{4}$" seam allowance. A strip of binding can be used for the top and bottom, using the method described on page 7. The sides of the quilt will need separate strips and will need to be folded under to finish the ends. Fold the binding to the back and whipstitch in place.

QUILT ASSEMBLY DIAGRAM

Finished size 16" square

MATERIALS

- $\frac{1}{2}$ yard blue fabric
- $\frac{1}{2}$ yard turquoise fabric

CUTTING

1. From the blue fabric, cut one $16\frac{1}{2}$" square and two $2\frac{1}{2}$" squares. Cut the $2\frac{1}{2}$" squares diagonally for four triangles for the corner of the napkin.

2. From the turquoise fabric, cut one $16\frac{1}{2}$" square for back of the napkin, one 1" x 8" rectangle, and one $2\frac{1}{2}$" square. Cut the $2\frac{1}{2}$" square diagonally for two triangles.

ASSEMBLY

1. Lay out one turquoise fabric and three blue fabric A triangles as shown in Corner Unit Assembly Diagrams. Join one turquoise fabric and one blue fabric triangle. Join blue fabric triangles to turquoise fabric sides of the square to complete corner unit.

CORNER UNIT ASSEMBLY
DIAGRAMS

2. Center and sew the 1" x 8" turquoise fabric rectangle across the top of the unit. Press.

3. Join the unit to one corner of the blue print 16½" square. Trim and press.

4. Place front and back of the napkin with right sides together. Stitch a ¼" seam allowance, leaving an opening large enough to turn the napkin. Turn, press, and hand-stitch the opening closed.